The Choice of a Lifetime

The Choice of a Lifetime

What You Need to Know Before Adopting

Kyle N. Weir

NTI Upstream  Chicago

NTI Upstream
180 N. Michigan Avenue, Ste. 700
Chicago, Illinois 60601
Visit our website at www.ntiupstream.com

The names of children and families in clinical cases in *The Choice of a Lifetime* have been changed to protect their privacy.

Grateful acknowledgment is made to the following for use of published material:

"Figure 5.1," "Figure 5.2," and "Figure 5.3," were originally published as "Table 5.2 Parents' Behavior/Under the Behavior," "Table 5.1 Child's Behavior/Under the Behavior" in *Attachment-Focused Family Therapy*. © 2007 by Daniel A. Hughes. Used by permission of Daniel Hughes and W.W. Norton & Company, Inc.

"Figure 8.1," "Figure 8.2," and "Figure 8.3," were originally published in "Cultural Competence for Transracial Adoptive Parents" by Elizabeth Vonk in *Social Work*, Vol. 46, no. 3 (July 2001): 253-55. Used by permission of the National Association of Social Workers.

"Figures 9.1," "Figure 9.2" and "Figure 9.3" were originally published in *Coming Out of the Adoptive Closet* by Kyle N. Weir. © 2003 by University Press of America. Used by permission of University Press of America.

Chapter five contains a slightly revised version of "5 Steps to Transition," which originally appeared in *Parent Life*, 2009. Used by permission of Lifeway Christian Resources.

Front cover images used by permission of Alamy.

Cover Design by Natalie Smith
Interior Design by Annie Heckman
Edited by Jeff Link

ISBN: 978-0-615-42174-2
Printed in the United States of America
Library of Congress Control Number 2011920374

To my wife, Allison, who has been my support and partner in our adoption endeavors

And to our children,
Kellie, Nathan, Samantha, Joshua, Jason, and Danny

I shall be telling this with a sigh
Somewhere ages and ages hence:
Two roads diverged in a wood, and I—
I took the one less traveled by,
And that has made all the difference.

—Frost, *The Road Not Taken*

Foreword

This is a unique book. Some books talk "at" you from the professional perspective of the adoption researcher or therapist. Such a book leaves out the inside experience of what it is like to actually adopt a child into your family. Other books talk "to" you from the parent's perspective but leave out important discussions of attachment, trauma, and the rich theoretical foundation of knowledge about these topics. This book does it all. At once an adoption researcher, teacher, marriage and family therapist specializing in adopted families, and, if that weren't enough, a father of six adopted children, Kyle Weir is in a unique position to teach us about the adoption process—which is, indeed, the choice of a lifetime.

And Weir teaches us well. It is as though we are sitting with him in his home after a dinner meal, discussing the possibility of adopting. He does not seek to give us a picture of adoption through rose-colored glasses because that can easily lead to disillusionment and disappointment. Instead, Weir discusses, with real life examples, the successes and the challenges that parents can face adopting children from the domestic foster care system or internationally. He clarifies market forces in adoption and the staggering need in our country for families willing to open their home to a child not naturally born to them. We learn about the many roads to adoption and the diversity that exists among adoptable children. Weir teaches us about the effects of early trauma on the child and what families should be prepared for when bringing such a child home.

Unlike some, Weir doesn't want us to enter into adoption naively thinking that love is enough and that any child will eventually fit right in. He also doesn't want us to be so swept away by our wish for a child or by the needs of a parentless child that we rush to say "yes" when we should say, "Wait and think." Weir wants us to ask ourselves hard questions about ourselves and our family's strengths, values, and limitations, and he hopes we answer them just as he has written this book: honestly and openly. Parents who take his "homework" seriously will be more likely to have successful adoptions and to be fulfilled by them. This will bode well for the many children who come into "forever homes." As children of informed parents, they, indeed, will be there forever with parents who will embrace the children as their own and will stick with them should the going get rough. This is the nature of forever, and ensuring such permanence is the purpose of the book.

At the same time we learn of the risks and concerns of adoption, we also learn from Weir that there is help for us as we try to help our child. He discusses available options for therapy and writes from his own professional experience about what works best. This is another place in the book where we reap the benefits of Weir's role as a professional. His discussion of therapy options will be a huge help to parents who often do not appreciate the differences between therapy approaches or realize that the focus on attachment and trauma is crucial. Please don't skip the last chapter in this book. It is the icing on the cake, a call to action with words of caution and the sharing of a touching personal story of Weir's family. It is the open sharing of Weir's personal experiences in his family that brings his points home. He speaks to us from the heart of a dad. We can feel his commitment to adoption as a valued, even cherished way to become a family, and we can feel the depth of that connection, rivaling any created through blood ties. This is both a warm comfortable book and a book that does not mince words or try to convince us that we should adopt. Weir wants us think deeply and thoroughly about our adoption possibilities so that, if we do decide to adopt, things will be more likely to go well. This is what we all want and need from adoption: a family in which we feel loved, wanted, secure, and to which we know we will always belong. For adoption is, truly, the choice of a lifetime.

Phyllis B. Rubin, Psy.D.
Author of the book *Play with Them: Theraplay Groups in the Classrooms*

Acknowledgments

At times this book has seemed as though it were the work of a lifetime. From an overly ambitious and encyclopedic work that sought to divulge everything I've ever learned about adoption to anyone willing to listen (e.g., prospective adoptive parents, adoptive parents, marriage and family therapists, counselors, social workers, psychologists, students in clinical training programs, and educators), this book has been honed to reach a specific audience—prospective adoptive couples sorting through the wide range of adoption options available to them.

I am indebted to a host of people for making this book possible. My wife and children are intricately linked to this endeavor. Their support during the numberless hours I spent writing, the dozens of times I asked Allison to read early drafts, and the numerous weekends they spent out of town visiting extended family to allow me to work uninterrupted has been invaluable. Like me, they know the purpose of this book—to help other families realize the joy of adoption we've experienced as a family. Adoption has been a God-given gift to us, and we want to share that gift with your family.

My clinical experiences as a therapist and social worker have informed this book, and I am deeply grateful for all that I have learned from my clients about adoption. Without access to their personal experiences and stories this book would not exist. The faculty, staff, and students in the Counselor Education program at California State University, Fresno, also have been of tremendous assistance in this work. In particular, I'd like to thank Phyllis Rubin, who has taken the lead in working with me to facilitate the coordination of the Whole Family Theraplay project at the Fresno Family Counseling Center. I cannot express, enough, my gratitude for her guidance, friendship, and support.

I also wish to express my gratitude for the guidance and direction of the publishing staff at NTI Upstream. Jeff Link, my patient editor, has provided energy and excitement when I needed it, tempered my academic tone, and helped me write in a voice accessible to adoptive parents seeking answers to questions about adoption for the first time. Finally, I am appreciative of you, the reader. Your desire to be informed about the choices available to you gives me hope for the tens of thousands of children in need of an adoptive home.

Contents

Introduction

It was June 11, 1994, when I heard my wife Allison on the phone with Julie, a single teen mom we knew from church. By the gist of the conversation, I knew things weren't going well. We'd been over to see Julie and her baby, Kellie, the night before, and it sounded like things weren't any better in the light of day. Julie was overwhelmed; what teenager wouldn't be?

With our marriage just beginning, Allison and I were not yet trying to adopt. Allison worked as the director of a day care center in a residential home for teen moms, and I was still trying to finish my undergraduate program at the University of Southern California and get into graduate school. When the bishop of our church asked us to help out with a pregnant teen in the congregation, it only seemed natural since Allison already had experience working with teen mothers. We became very close to Julie during the first few months of our marriage, and her daughter Kellie was born in mid-May. In her first weeks as a mother, Julie was having a hard time emotionally. At such a young age, she didn't know how to be a mother. She was still dealing with her own emotional development and needed to time to solidify her identity and figure herself out. We tried to be supportive. Every few nights we'd visit Julie at her parents' home. While Allison counseled Julie about parenting and Julie's own emotional needs, I'd hold Kellie and sing to her. In a strange way, I felt incredibly close to this child who wasn't even mine.

That morning when I heard Allison say we'd be right over, I had a sixth sense about what would happen. And sure enough, five minutes later, we were holding Kellie and our lives were forever changed. What I had thought would be temporary babysitting relief for the weekend turned out to be an eternal commitment to a daughter whom I love dearly. In reality, it took much longer than five minutes for the relationship to become permanent. For three years Kellie went back and forth between our home and Julie's before we finally had the privilege of adopting her. But my personal journey into adoptive parenthood had begun, and with it, my professional endeavor into adoptive studies as a marriage and family therapist.

Our story is hardly exceptional. Contemporary adoptive families are more complex and diverse than ever before as traditional representations of social and family structure, racial composition, and methods of adoption have broadened over the last quarter of a century. The rise in divorced, single-parented, and grandparent-led families has brought with it changes in the types of adoptive families we find in cities and towns throughout the country. Modern day adoptive families comprise children of different nationalities, children who are older or who have specialized medical needs, children who have troubling foster and prenatal care histories that complicate their development. This, of course, means more choices for would-be adoptive parents. As a prospective parent, you'll have to consider how much contact you wish to have with the birth family, what countries you wish to target in your adoptive search, and the child's racial background and medical or behavioral needs. And these, as I'm sure you've guessed, are only the tip of the iceberg.

My hope is that this book will be useful for prospective adoptive couples and single parents who are seeking a reliable, research-based text to assist them in making informed decisions about adoption. Often couples feel overwhelmed at first by the vast amounts of forms, trainings, and procedures required for approval. Later, they feel discouraged by statements social workers and other adoption service providers make about the availability of children. The types of adoptive family forms, adoptive children, adoptive methods, and adoptive lifestyle choices that are available to them only become clear at late stages in the decision making process. As a result, many couples are left scratching their heads, uncertain about which direction is best suited to their needs.

The reality is that most prospective adoptive couples choose a method of adoption based on limited evidence. On the basis of a friend's recommendation (which is not a bad place to start) they get involved with a particular agency or method of adoption, even though it may not be right for them. Dissatisfied, they nonetheless feel obliged to continue with the agency or method because they have already gone through paperwork, fingerprinting, and other exhausting procedures and do not want to start the process all over again. Hopefully, this book will ease that process. Before committing time and expense to a particular adoption agency, you'll be able to familiarize yourself with a number of the options available to you and your family.

The book is organized into three sections. The first offers an introduction into various methods of adoption and the types of children available through these methods. The second enumerates several research-based factors affecting adoption outcomes so you'll be better equipped to make informed choices if you do decide to enter the adoption market. Periodically throughout the book, I also try to highlight my own personal and clinical experiences with adoption where these stories can be instructive or meaningful. In the final section, I advance a rationale for more families to consider adopting children.

Above all, this book is intended to educate and support newly adoptive couples as they make the rewarding transition to parenthood. Parents adopting for the first time often experience similar feelings, whether this be the welcome joy of meeting a new family member for the first time or the trepidation of getting to know a child's unique habits and passions. If your family is anything like ours, these feelings will include a mixture of contradictory emotions ranging from stress and frustration to relief and hope. As one of several resources in your adoptive journey, I hope this book will help you find success and fulfillment in the formative period when you first bring a new child into your lives.

Chapter One
Social and Legal Changes Affecting Adoption

Historically, adoption has been a tool to solve two social problems: couples seeking a child due to infertility, and children in need of a family because they are without proper, available parents. A small percentage of couples adopt for reasons other than fertility problems, such as the desire to give a needy child a home or to provide a caretaker for kin within an extended family, but the majority of couples in the United States come to adoption because of their own infertility. Some couples have never been able to have a child, what is known as *primary infertility*. Others have previously given birth to one or more children, but now are unable to conceive or carry a child full term (*secondary infertility*) and seek to add to the number of children in their family. Traditionally, whenever a child in need of a family and an infertile couple have come together through adoption, the social community has applauded the connection as a "win-win."

However, in the latter half of the twentieth century, this began to change. With more reported cases of infertility came increased demand for adoptable children and a shrinking supply of certain "preferred" categories of adoptable babies and children.[1] Problems arose as the availability of healthy, white infants dwindled at the same time the number of African-American children who needed homes spiked.[2] Unfortunately, this imbalance persists today. Although a growing number of

African-American couples are seeking adoption, most prospective adoptive couples are white and tend to adopt within their race. As a matter of fact, one government-sponsored study of successful adoptive families in 2007 found that the number of Caucasian-parented families was as high as 80 percent.[3] In short, these trends mean that the greatest demand among adoptive parents is for healthy, Caucasian infants at the same time the supply of these children is declining. Like in any economic market, when demand increases and supply declines, a predicament is in the offing.

The Commoditization of Adoptive Children

It is an unfortunate truth that the availability of adoptable children depends on the characteristics of child a prospective couple desires. But why are healthy, white infants in such short supply? If you suspected other factors—besides the fact that the majority of adoptive parents happen to be white—contributed to this imbalance, you were exactly right. Since the 1960s there has been a sharp decrease in the number of healthy, Caucasian infants whose birth mothers make an *adoption plan*. This was due, in part, to the increase in abortions following Roe v. Wade in 1973 and the widespread availability of birth control, both of which meant fewer women were having children.[4] Above that, more mothers were choosing single parenthood because of the increased acceptance they found in the social community. Presently, the demand for healthy, Caucasian infants, particularly females, is the greatest, but these children are the least available for adoption. Deciding to adopt a child who fits this description often means long waiting periods and expensive adoption procedures.

However, if you are willing to modify your desires to match the supply of children in the adoption pool, the opportunities to adopt increase, the waiting period is generally much shorter, and the legal procedures associated with adoption often cost less. As a prospective parent, this may mean broadening your child search to include minority children, children with histories of abuse/neglect, children prenatally exposed to drugs and alcohol, older children, and children with other medical or special needs. In expanding your search, you won't be alone: many couples already are making such choices, turning to transracial adoptions, international adoptions, and other methods of adopting as a response to market forces and the supply of adoptable children.

Of course referring to children as a "supply" is uncomfortable to most of us, as it should be. But like it or not, in the adoption market, adoptable children are increasingly becoming the sought-after resource, in what is called the *commoditization of adoptive children.* Prospective adoptive couples seek to have a child and, like in any economic model, if what they initially desire is not available, too expensive, or too difficult to obtain, they modify their desires for something that is more affordable, more available, and easier to obtain. A good approach is to consider your preference about the characteristics of the adopted child you seek to adopt relative to the time factors, cost factors, and availability that exist in the pool of prospective adoptable children.[5]

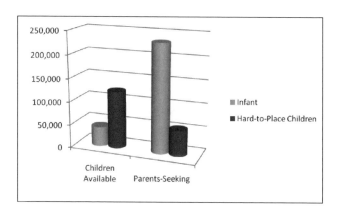

FIGURE 1.1 Supply of adoptable children in relation to parental demand

The Deinstitutionalization of Adoption

The shrinking role of institutionalization is another crucial factor affecting the adoption market. Historically, the adoption of children has happened through institutions. In early America through the mid-twentieth century, orphanages were the primary institutions where prospective adoptive couples sought a child. Most of us are familiar with the musical *Annie*, the story of a young redhead who lived in an orphanage until Daddy Warbucks adopted her and brought her to his home. As a reflection of the harsh conditions of early adoptive institutions, the tale is not entirely fanciful. In the mid-to-latter parts of the nineteenth century, children from orphanages in the eastern United States were often subject to poor sanitation and rigid authority. Many were brought across the country on crowded trains, making stops in small towns in the west, where pastors and priests facilitated adoptions to local couples.

Later, in the mid-to-latter twentieth century, foster care and child welfare agencies became the norm. Although these agencies arose in an effort to deinstitutionalize the adoptive process for needy children, the reality was they did little but exchange one form of institutionalization for another. Agencies were rigid in their policies and almost uniformly prohibited transracial adoptions, foster parent adoptions, and adoptions allowing open visitation with the child's biological parents. Although medical doctors and lawyers performed a small number of independent adoptions, even these well-meaning pioneers subscribed to the institutionalized patterns, ethical codes, and standard operating procedures of the day. As a rule, it has been American adoptive practice to turn to institutions when seeking to adopt.

However, in the last two decades, we've witnessed in adoption what we've come to see as emblematic of the modern era: the crumbling of public confidence in institutions. Now families are seeking their own way of living an adoptive family life, without the rules, formality, or supervision of traditional out-lets. Adoptive parents, birth mothers, and adopted children—the so-called *adoption triad*—who for decades have followed the policies of agencies with little choice or flexibility, have much greater autonomy in how, where, and whom they adopt. In an earlier work, I describe this as follows:

> [*Deinstitutionalization*] seems to stem from members of the adop-tion triad seeking a better 'fit' with their own needs in the adop-tion process, as compared to the institutionally prescribed notions of how adoption is supposed to work. The current emphasis is on a negotiated adoption process that fits the adoption triad members' needs rather than a bureaucratic, dogmatic approach to adoption set forth by the rules and regulations of adoption agencies and institutions.[6]

The main point is that deinstitutionalization may open doors for you that would otherwise be closed. When Allison and I were beginning to adopt our first child, Kellie, we need-ed to find an agency that would facilitate the adoption. We had an unusual circumstance in that we already had found a birth mother and child on our own; we just needed an agency to facilitate the adoption. (Now we call these types of adop-tions *designated adoptions*.) One agency refused to complete the adoption because we already knew the birth mother and wanted her to be a part of the child's life; that is, we wanted an *open adoption*. Specializing in *closed adoptions*—in which the birth parent does not have contact with the child—the agency wanted Julie to select from a list of prospective adoptive couple profiles and to place Kellie with one of their couples already awaiting a child. When Julie told them that she wasn't com-fortable placing her child with a family she didn't know, the agency said they couldn't help us.

Everything changed in the adoption world just a few years later, in 1997, with the passage of the Adoption and Safe Fami-lies Act (ASFA). An agency that was so unwilling to bend its rules during the pre-1997 era when we were adopting Kellie now has become incredibly flexible, going to great lengths to make adoptions work for the interests of the adoption triad parties involved. They now do open adoptions and designated adoptions, in addition to more traditional adoptions. Why? Because market forces make it necessary—forces that, as we shall see, are shaped in no small part by ASFA.

The Adoption and Safe Families Act of 1997

From a legal standpoint, ASFA made significant changes to the U.S. child welfare system.[7] First, the Act identified the child's health and welfare as the "paramount concern" of those making decisions regarding children in American foster care or child welfare systems. That signaled a critical shift in U.S. adoption policy from a framework rooted in parental rights to one designed to protect children and encourage permanent living arrangements inside adoptive homes. As part of this effort, the legislation reduced the time required for "reasonable efforts" toward reunification with a biological parent or parents before a child is freed for adoption. Before ASFA of 1997 federal law did not require states to begin termination of parental rights proceedings based on the length of the child's stay in foster care. Under the new law, states are required to terminate parental rights on behalf of any child who has been in foster care for 15 out of the most recent 22 months. This provision also allows for dual or *concurrent planning,* meaning a child can be placed in an adoptive or permanent home while reunification services are underway. These new requirements signified a dramatic shift in U.S. adoption practice, allowing children to be adopted at younger ages and increasing the amount of children available for adoption. Finally, the Act authorized $20 million for each of fiscal years 1999–2003 for payments to eligible states for each child who is adopted (or has other similar permanent plans arranged) from the foster care rolls. This is known as *permanency planning.* According to the Act, the amount of the bonus is $4,000 for each foster child adopted and $6,000 for each adoption of a child with special needs; states are required to provide health insurance coverage to any special-needs child for whom an adoption assistance agreement has been created. These changes, along with other important aspects of ASFA, have appreciably altered the face of adoption and child welfare services over the last dozen years.

Public child welfare agencies have been affected enormously by the legislation, in large part because of AFSA's focus on the government's responsibility to "at risk" children. Part of this responsibility means ensuring these children live in a safe home with mature, capable caretakers. Greater attention to the unfit living conditions that at-risk children often endure has led, in turn, to an increase in the number of children available for adoption. Estimates place the current number of available adoptable children on the child welfare rolls somewhere from 114,000 to 115,000 out of the approximately 424,000 children currently in public care.[8]

It is worth pointing out that research generally supports the efficacy of policies outlined in ASFA. One such study by Emily Kernan and Jennifer Lansford at Duke University's Center for Child and Family Policy summarizes the benefits of the legislation succinctly:

> Developmental research suggests that foster care often results in better outcomes for children than does reunification with their biological families but that adoption often leads to better outcomes than does foster care. These findings indicate that the overall goals outlined in ASFA are appropriate and likely serve the best interests of many children.[9]

Then again, while ASFA 1997 is an important first step in guaranteeing the best interest of children, improving the lives of children also demands a sense of moral responsibility from prospective parents. Building on the success of ASFA, we need more prospective adoptive parents who are willing to modify their preferences to include the physical, racial, and medical characteristics of children who are already available. Be realistic and honest with yourself about what you can and cannot handle in an adoption experience, but recognize that the need is great. By expressing that you are willing to modify your preferences to suit the "supply" of children available, you may be providing a home for a child who might otherwise remain on the child welfare rolls for a lengthy, possibly indefinite, period of time.

Summary

There have been so many changes in the world of adoption, particularly since the passage of the Adoption and Safe Families Act in 1997. As a prospective adoptive couple or single parent, it may be a little overwhelming to consider all the information you have to account to make the right decision for you and your family. Understanding the changes described in this chapter hopefully will give you some basic knowledge as to how to proceed. As you begin the adoptive search, keep in mind how changes in the supply of and demand for different kinds of children have led to the commoditization of adoptable children. Be sure to consider the various factors that go into the adoption process, including the kind of child you desire (i.e., race, health, history, and age) as well as the time, cost, and effort you are willing to expend to adopt such a child. Ideally, this first chapter has kept you open to the idea of modifying your desires toward adoptable children who are more available. The next chapter focuses on different agencies and kinds of adoption, including methods of how to go about adopting a child.

Chapter Two
Adoption Methods and the Myth of Disruption

Couples will select a method of adoption for a variety of reasons: convenience, affordability, availability of a specific child or desired type of child, or referral from a friend or colleague. But the main reason is because they have confidence that the method will prevent later separation with the child. In fact one of the most common beliefs affecting parents' choice of an adoption method is that the preferred method comes with the "least risk"—meaning the least risk of adoption disruption, or risk that the child will be reclaimed by the birth family. In a study for my previous book, most families, regardless of the type of adoption method they chose, confessed they made their choice for this very reason. I would come from a domestic private agency adoption household, for instance, to a household in which the family had chosen to adopt internationally, only to find each family claiming their method of adoption had the least chance of disruption. Obviously, many of these views were misinformed. In reality there has been little evidence to suggest which methods of adoption have higher or lower rates of disruption, although we do know that adoption disruption rates tend to be comparatively low in the United States.

While it is true there are some risks associated with the adoption process, the *perception* of risk is often higher than the *actual* risks. The National Adoption Information Clearinghouse reports that 80 percent of adoptions remain intact before finalization, and that 98 percent are not dissolved after legalization.[1] In addition, we now know that the age of placement, the child's behavioral and attachment history, and the presence or absence of special needs seem to be key indicators of adoption disruption and dissolution.[2] Encouragingly, less than 1 percent of infant adoptions disrupt, 10–12 percent of adoptions disrupt when the age of placement is 3 or older, and 14.3 percent disrupt when children with special needs of any age are adopted.[3] On the whole, these adoption disruption and dissolution rates suggest strong patterns of family stability among adoptive families in the United States.

Nevertheless, the widespread perception is that adoption comes at a high risk. Rare events such as the "Baby Jessica" and "Baby Richard" cases of the early 1990s attract the media's attention, prompting horror stories of adoption disruptions to reverberate through the community.[4] What is less obvious is how exceptional these cases tend to be. In both the "Baby Jessica" and "Baby Richard" case, the biological mothers consented to the adoption of their child. However they did so duplicitously. Baby Jessica's mother failed to notify the biological father of the paternity of the child. Baby Richard's mother lied, claiming the baby had died when he had lived, to deprive the birth father the right to seek custody. Later, when the biological mothers reconciled with the biological fathers, they sought to "undo" the adoptions. However, in both instances, the birth fathers' paternity rights were never properly surrendered.

As we learned, the early 1990s was a different era for adoption: ASFA had yet to make adoption and permanency planning a key social goal. However, even for the time, these cases were egregious departures from standard adoption practices. You can rest assured that adoption practices and adoption law today are far more meticulous about securing the birth mother's (or father's) parental consent prior to terminating the parental rights of the biological parents.

The term *adoption disruption,* sometimes called a "failed adoption,"³ refers to the termination of an adoption and removal of the adoptee from the adoptive parents' home before the adoption process is legally finalized. Sometimes adoption disruptions are initiated by the birth parents reclaiming their child. Other times they occur when adoptive parents decide, generally because of the child's behavior problems, that they cannot continue with the adoption.

Adoption dissolution, on the other hand, refers to an adoption that fails after legal finalization. Dissolutions are similar to disruptions in some ways. Like disruptions, they often are set in motion by adoptive parents who can no longer care for the child.

FIGURE 2.1 Adoption disruption and dissolution

The reality is that regardless of the adoption method you choose, there is a very good chance you will never have to worry about disruption. Still, knowing where, how, and with what method to start the adoption process can be confusing, and distinctions among methods are certainly important. Many of the differences in adoptive families stem from how adoptive parents seek to establish custody of the child. Throughout this chapter, we will use the term *method of adoption* to describe the means through which the couple adopts a child, whether this is through an agency or an independent outlet. Below are some of the most common methods:

- Public child welfare agency
- Domestic private adoption agency
- International private adoption agency
- Independent / professionals (lawyers and medical doctors)

- Internet / designated adoptions (which require the services of lawyers through the court process)
- Kinship / stepfamily adoptions
- Combinations of these methods

Before making a commitment, it is important to familiarize yourself with the basic features of these methods and attend orientation meetings from multiple, diverse agencies. Each orientation is an educational exercise. The more educated you become about the different methods of adoption, agencies, and their practices, the better you will be able to make an informed decision that matches your family's needs and desires. As you might expect, adoptions are more successful (i.e., less likely to disrupt) if the prospective adoptive couple is educated and has spent time in thoughtful consideration regarding the contingencies of possible adoptions and the best fit for their family.

Domestic Private Agency Adoptions

Domestic private agencies are one of the most common sites of adoption in the United States, estimated to oversee 37.5 percent of all U.S. adoptions.[6] These agencies may include not-for-profit, profit-seeking, and religiously affiliated adoption agencies. Couples who are committed to adopting a healthy, white infant may have a slightly higher probability of doing so through domestic private agencies, but the wait is generally long and the process can be expensive. Generally, these agencies rely on birth mothers and fathers to voluntarily relinquish their parental rights. This is different from public child welfare agency adoptions, in which parental rights are more likely to be terminated in court due to parental abuse, neglect, or child abandonment.

As part of private agency adoption, birth family members are generally offered counseling or therapy at the expense of the adopting couple. Should you choose to adopt through a domestic agency, be sure to factor these costs into your budget, as well as costs for the birth mother's pregnancy, delivery, and child care expenses.

Each state varies in its definition of what is legally allowed, as well as what is mandated, concerning payment for expenses. The spirit of such legal scrutiny is to ensure that prospective adopting couples are not "paying for a child," a practice which is illegal. Approximately forty-five states and several U.S. territories regulate allowable birth parent expenses.[7] For example, in California, an adopting couple may pay a birth mother's expenses for items related to the pregnancy such as a stipend for groceries, housing costs consistent with the birth mother's lifestyle, medical costs, and other similar expenses. They may not buy a car or other lavish gifts, but they may help with minor repairs to a car or with gasoline for medical care visits for the pregnancy. Other states such as Alabama, Indiana, Maine, and Wisconsin have statutes similar to California. A few states simply cap the overall dollar amount allowed: Arizona ($1,000), Connecticut ($1,500), Idaho ($2,000), Indiana ($3,000), and Wisconsin ($1,000), while a handful of states—Hawaii, Massachusetts, Nebraska, Rhode Island, and some U.S. territories— do not address birth parent expenses in statute, making it virtually illegal to pay for them.[8]

Historically, these agencies tend to specialize in finding children high in demand but scarce in availability. This is one of the reasons why they are so widely used—and why they are comparatively expensive.

Public Child Welfare Adoptions

The Adoption and Safe Families Act of 1997 has helped to make more children available for adoption, but generally the children have histories of abuse or neglect, abandonment, or other special needs. Additionally, the majority of these children are ethnic minorities.

When we apply the commoditization model from earlier we find that child welfare agencies have a large supply of children available for adoption, yet the demand for these children remains low. As a result, the adoption experiences of families who go through public child welfare agencies often stand in stark contrast to those of families who use domestic private adoptions agencies. The outcomes and clinical needs of the adopted children also vary, as we will see. But despite the potential challenges of adopting through one of the public child welfare agencies, doing so can be a rewarding way of creating an adoptive family. Many children from public child welfare agencies, in spite of their difficult histories, respond well to the love, structure, and security of a good adoptive home. At first these children may shirk from the love and care they receive because it is vastly different from the harmful environments of their origin. Accordingly, the adjustment period may take longer—sometimes years. And it may be fraught with behavioral challenges. In the long run, though, children respond to a balanced set of good parenting dimensions.*

Some positive aspects of public adoptions should be highlighted here. To begin with, couples willing to adopt older or special-needs children can often obtain rapid placement of a child, after just a few months of training and the proper completion of background checks. They can also expect—and should demand if it is not happening—visits from social workers to help with emotional and behavioral challenges that may

---

* The "balanced" dimensions of good parenting are explained in further detail in chapter 10. Here I discuss attachment theory and a specific type of play therapy called Theraplay, which I have utilized in clinical work and research with adoptive families. Essentially, these dimensions of a healthy parent-child relationship include a balance of structure (listening to and following directions from an adult in charge), engagement (paying attention to a child in a playful, enjoyable way), nurture (tender, loving interactions), and challenge (facing and overcoming challenges together).

arise. Furthermore, children from public child welfare agencies qualify for medical and dental benefits, which generally include mental health or therapy coverage. Adoptive families are advised to use these benefits to see a family therapist, and many do; this is one reason why adopted children tend to go to therapy more.

Another advantage of public adoption is that couples receive a small stipend to help cover some of the child's expenses prior to the finalization of the adoption. Families also may qualify for the federally funded Adoptions Assistance Program (AAP), which typically continues the benefits received in foster care until the child reaches maturity. Finally, and perhaps most importantly, there is the intrinsic reward of helping a child that is genuinely in need. These children are often disadvantaged due to mistreatment, neglect, or other special needs, and need a good home that will provide therapeutic support.

At present there are literally thousands of children in need of permanent adoptive family placements. In their book *Risk and Promise,* Ira Chasnoff and his colleagues at the Children's Research Triangle in Chicago describe a growing trend toward transracial adoption in the context of the public welfare system. Noting the growing number of African-American children who are available for adoption, the authors point out that there are "not enough African-American homes available to welcome the tens of thousands of same-race children into foster care or adoption."[9] One leading organization in the child welfare movement, the Child Welfare League of America, estimates that 40 percent of children waiting to be adopted in the child welfare systems across the nation are African American.[10] Increased effort must be made within the adoption community to encourage prospective parents to consider transracial adoption as a way to meet this existing need.

International Private Agency Adoptions

In the last few years, celebrities such as Angelina Jolie and Madonna have attracted a good deal of media attention to the issue of international adoption. Indeed, it is hard to shop at the grocery store without being exposed to tabloids at the checkout stand announcing the latest international adoption by such celebrities. However this method of adoption is utilized much less than you would probably suspect. According to a report of the U.S. Census Bureau, only about 5 percent of U.S. adoptions are international adoptions. About half of these families adopt children from Asia, mostly from China, South Korea, and more recently Vietnam. The remainder is largely divided between Latin America (33%) and Europe (16%).[11]

International adoptions generally involve a private agency or facilitator in the United States to prepare the dossier, conduct background checks, complete the home study, and make connections with an agency or facilitator in the child's home country. Countries vary in their restrictions on age, financial status, marital status, sexual orientation, health, and ancestry, and if you are interested in adopting internationally a good place to begin your search is the U.S. Department of State's intercountry adoption website available at http://www.adoption.state.gov/. It is important to stay as current as possible when seeking information, for in the midst of adoption, political relations between countries can shift, and laws and policies may change.

Most countries require the adopting couple to spend at least a few weeks in the child's country of origin. Many countries require a parent to personally travel with the child to their new homeland, and in some countries, parents are required to legally adopt the child in the host country before they can bring the child to the United States. Upon return, parents must again go through the legal process of adoption in their home state. In the past, adopting U.S. couples had some issues with the immigration status of their internationally adopted child, but the Child Citizenship Act of 2000 has largely smoothed out immigration status problems, so that children legally adopted by U.S. citizens become citizens automatically.[12]

Countries are always concerned about the possibility of child trafficking. In developing countries, especially, there exists the temptation to steal children from biological parents and "sell" them to American couples who often have no knowledge the child was stolen. Unfortunately most countries do not have any organized mechanism to deal with this dilemma and, generally, when this problem because pervasive, the response of the host country is to cease allowing international adoptions.

As a rule, host countries want to ensure that parents are adopting the child for legitimate religious, humanitarian, or familial purposes and not for baser motives. Many countries require a post-placement home visit by a social worker to ensure children are safe and not being exploited in their new environment. As a response to this issue and other problems stemming from international adoptions, the Hague Conference on Private International Law developed a report called the *Convention of Protection of Children and Co-operation in Respect of Intercountry Adoption*. The key objectives, described in Article 1, are reproduced below:[13]

    a. to establish safeguards to ensure that intercountry adoptions take place in the best interests of the child and with respect for his or her fundamental rights as recognized in international law;

    b. to establish a system of co-operation amongst Contracting States to ensure that those safeguards are respected and thereby prevent the abduction, the sale of, or traffic in children;

    c. to secure the recognition in Contracting States of adoptions made in accordance with the Convention.

Despite the good intentions of the Hague Conference,

progress enforcing these laws will take time. Parents should be aware that there can be serious developmental, cognitive, and medical risks associated with international adoption. Some countries outside of the United States continue the practice of orphanages and these vary dramatically in physical condition, care and nurturance to children, record keeping, as well as in their medical care and childcare philosophies. As Schwartz points out in the *Handbook of Family Development and Intervention*, one of the real concerns for internationally adopted children is the amount of "pre-adoptive care" they received prior to adoption:

> Were children in an orphanage given enough food, affectionate handling, and exercise? Is the information on the birth parents complete in terms of health problems, substance abuse, prenatal care, and nutrition? How long has the child been in institutional or foster care? . . . Birthdates were often missing, itemized diagnoses and medications were unfamiliar to American physicians, children had apparently not been properly immunized against a variety of diseases ranging from polio to rubella, and there was often developmental delay in the adoptees unaccounted for in the available documents. . . . Children coming from the orphanages in what had been the Soviet Union should initially, at least, be regarded as children with special needs. Many of them certainly have memories of parents as well as the orphanage since these children may not be infants, and they may have been traumatized by the loss of parents in wartime. Another problem, more of legal concern, is whether the child was, perhaps, taken from the mother without her agreement.[14]

Children coming from such experiences often have serious medical and therapeutic treatment needs. Thankfully, families adopting internationally typically have the financial means to improve the child's economic well-being through adoption. That translates into better access to healthcare, a more nutritious diet, and increased educational opportunities.

Despite the healing that takes place in good adoptive

homes, it is necessary to be aware that identity issues typically arise in international adoptions. Usually this is due to a transracial component, and the child's natural curiosity about their birth origins. While adoptive parents may welcome the fact the child's birth parents are typically less involved in international adoption, meaning a lower risk of adoption disruption, they should be prepared to address the challenges of ethnic and cultural identity.

Independent Adoptions

Independent adoptions have become another popular method of adoption. One of the advantages of independent adoptions is their flexibility. Adoption triad members can negotiate an adoption scenario that fits their needs rather than being required to subscribe to agency policies. Sometimes the adoption facilitator, often a professional such as a doctor or lawyer, has contacts with hospitals, teen group homes, or an extended social network and assists in finding a child for the couple. More often independent adoptions involve adoption triad members finding children on their own. This can be facilitated through social network contacts, the Internet, e-mails, or other contacts. In some cases, prospective adoptive couples do mass mailings hoping to find someone who knows someone in need of placing a child into an adoptive home. Occasionally those types of mailing lead to a significant contact and an adoption, but more often they highlight the scarcity of highly desired children.

Be forewarned, the advantage of flexibility in independent adoptions also comes with risk. Because there is less structure, there is greater chance for fraud. Birth mothers have been known to promise their children to a couple over the Internet, only for the couple to discover that the mother has made the same arrangements with another unsuspecting family hoping to get the "best deal." With independent adoptions, the adage of "caveat emptor" or "let the buyer beware" is sound advice.

Independent adoption costs range from relatively cheap to incredibly expensive. Because lawyers tend to bill on an hourly basis, you should expect the cost to increase considerably, as legal concerns arise. Under extreme circumstances a case may cost as much as $50,000. However for a simple procedure the story may be very different. For a couple already utilizing an agency, hiring a lawyer to speed the adoption along when it comes time for a court hearing, may cost as little as $400.

Kinship and Stepfamily Adoptions

Kinship and stepfamily adoptions make up 42 percent of all U.S. adoptions.[15] This includes adoptions by a stepparent, formal or legal adoptions by grandparents or other relatives, and informal adoptions by the extended kin system of the birth family. As a rule, this type of adoption is radically different from the methods previously discussed. It may or may not be subject to legal sanction, although the process is increasingly falling under legal scrutiny.

When a family member, such as a grandparent or stepparent does not legally adopt the child but provides care for them we call it an *informal adoption*. If a grandparent, stepparent, or other family member legally adopts the child, it is termed a *formal adoption* or *formal kinship adoption*.

When grandparents, stepparents, or other kin legally adopt, there is generally still some social connection to the birth parent. In stepparent adoptions, usually one of the biological parents must give up parental rights. Sometimes issues arise concerning contact with biological parents' relatives—the child's grandparents, for example. Many families will work out such arrangements informally, for according to Schwartz "courts vary in how they resolve questions about the resulting visitation rights of these biological relatives."[16] To standardize responses to these concerns, some states have changed their adoption laws to allow continued post-adoption visits if the biological relative has already established a relationship with the child. More grandparents are taking on the role of primary parent to their grandchildren. In such cases, children may still maintain contact with birth parents; and there is generally a relationship between the grandmother and the parent of the adopted grandchild. This is not new—in fact, it has been a practice for centuries. What is different in the contemporary practice is that the adoption is becoming legally formalized; the traditional view of grandparenting as a time to "spoil" the grandchild, leaving the structure and discipline up to the parents is slowly eroding.[17] Now in many households when parents are not functioning or absent, the grandparent has to play both roles. This is particularly challenging when age, health, and finances become unstable. It is an added struggle when daily caregiving becomes a full-time responsibility instead of the part-time experience many grandparents enjoy.

With informal adoptions by kin, the time period for the "adoption" may not be construed as permanent. Boundaries, including legal authority, custody, and consent issues, may be unclear in such arrangements and may shift with time. Nancy Boyd-Franklin, a psychologist at Rutgers University and the author of *Black Families in Therapy: A Multisystems Approach,* holds that informal adoptions are part of the normative "reciprocity of goods and services" that has long been a part of African-American culture.[18] According to Boyd-Franklin, it is not uncommon for ethnic minorities to be more likely than Caucasian families to embrace informal adoption. While Caucasian families do adopt at times within their kinship system, they are more likely to formalize the process legally.

Summary
Couples wanting to adopt seem to have one thing in common: they want a child to become a permanent part of their family.

Yet significant differences exist in how the family finds a child and formalizes the legal process to make their family relationships binding and permanent. Although the statistical odds of an adoption being disrupted are very low, the perception that adoption involves great risk remains high due to inordinate amounts of media attention given to the extremely rare cases where adoptions are disrupted or dissolved. With so many choices for selecting a child, from private adoption agencies, to public child welfare agency adoptions, to international, independent, and kinship adoptions, the best counsel I can give is for you to determine what kind of experience you are seeking (e.g., Do you want a younger or older child? Would you consider a child in need of special care?) and then attend orientation meetings at a variety of agencies.

Educate yourself about the kinds of adoptions available to you in your local area. As you speak with social workers, therapists, and other adoption facilitator professionals at the end of the orientation meetings, be clear about what kind of adoption experience you are looking for. Ask what kinds of adoptions the agency provides and request referrals to other types of agencies (especially if the organization seems to be providing something different than what you are after). While there's a scarcity of credible research regarding which method of adoption is "least risky" concerning adoption disruption, the method you select will have great bearing on the kind of child you receive into your home. Differing methods of adoption do lead to children of different races and ethnicities as well as children of vastly different prenatal and family histories. Our next chapter explores this wonderful diversity within adoptive families.

Chapter Three
Diversity Within Contemporary Adoptive Families

If you've ever been to a picnic or social event sponsored by an adoption or foster agency, one of the first things you'll notice is that you cannot automatically tell which children belong to which set of parents. One mother I interviewed for a previous book noticed this diversity at an adoption agency barbecue and called it "utopia."[1] Despite the diverse races and family constellations at the picnic, no one had to explain why his or her child had a different hair color or came from a different ethnic background. The adoptive parents I met felt accepted by their children regardless of variations in appearance. In fact, part of the reason why adoption is such a wonderful experience is because no two adoptive families are alike.

To be sure, the trend toward diversity within adoption is growing. As social stigmas about interracial marriages and relationships have declined, adoptions of children whose ethnicity, race, and heritage differ from the adoptive parents have become more socially acceptable. This has led to an increase in domestic transracial or cross-cultural adoptions, from 8 percent of total U.S. adoptions in 1993 to 17 percent by the time of the 2000 U.S. Census.[2] Additionally, international adoptions have grown to 5 percent of all U.S. adoptions, with about half coming from Asia, one-third from Latin America, and one-sixth from Europe.[3] When you combine the trends for domestic transracial adoptions and international adoptions, it is clear there is greater acceptance of racial and ethnic difference in adoption.

Of course racial or ethnic difference is not the only variation that exists within adoptive families. Diversity can also occur in the method of adoption, the level of openness (the amount of contact with birth family members), the family composition, and the presence or absence of children with special needs. Other factors such as the age of placement of the adopted child or children, the presence of biological sibling groups, and even how the adoptive family chooses to live and work contribute to the diversity that is found among adoptive families. Thus, as you consider adopting, it is important to have a good understanding of the extensive variety of adoptive family systems that exist and to make some critical choices at the onset. Particularly for couples or single parents considering adoption for the first time, it may be useful to answer the questions below to determine which type of adoptive family you wish to become.

- Is it essential for me/us to adopt an infant?
- How important is it to me that my child bear physical resemblance to me and/or my spouse?
- To what extent are my spouse and I comfortable with contact with my child's birth family members?
- Are we willing to take into our home multiple children or biological sibling groups?
- How would we handle boundary issues and other concerns of privilege if we chose to adopt from a relative or other family member in our kinship?
- How capable are we to raise a child diagnosed with behavioral problems, medical conditions, a history of abuse and neglect, or other special needs?
- How will others in our social network—extended family, friends, or co-workers for example—react to our adoption

decisions? What aspects or variations in adoption would our social community support or not support? How important is that support to us?

- How open will we be with our child and others when discussing adoption and adoption-related issues?
- How comfortable are we with being a "different" type of family through adoption?

Here it should be pointed out that diversity factors often vary according to the method of adoption. For example special needs and older ages of placement are typical of adoptions through public child welfare agencies. They can also be found in international adoptions or in independent adoptions. Transracial issues, on the other hand, may fit readily with international adoptions and domestic adoptions. As we look at diversity issues within adoption, keep in mind that the method in which you choose to adopt may play a role in the race and behavioral and medical needs of your child.

Transracial Adoptive Families

Adoptive parents who adopt children not of their own race or ethnicity, either from within their own country or internationally, are referred to as transracial adoptive parents. Domestically, transracial adoption grew out of the need to find more homes for waiting, available children. Several researchers have pointed to the concurrent trend, in the late twentieth century, of the declining number of available Caucasian babies and the escalating number of African American children needing an adoptive home.[4] Coupled with a lack of available same-race families ready to adopt, this imbalance created a surplus of African American children living as wards of the state. Additionally, Asian children who were orphaned during World War II, the Korean War, and Vietnam needed homes at a time when there were not a large number of Asian families able or willing to adopt children from these communities. Despite existing social prejudices, Caucasian couples began adopting minority children because of the convergence of social and market forces that made these children more readily attainable.

The practice of transracial adoption has been the subject of some controversy. In the popular 1995 film *Losing Isaiah*,[5] the debate is portrayed through the case example of a young African-American boy, Isaiah, abandoned by his mother who is addicted to crack cocaine. A white social worker at the hospital where Isaiah was taken after being found in a dumpster decides to adopt him. The birth mother goes into rehabilitation and begins to clean up her life. In the end there's a court battle for custody of Isaiah. The attorney representing the African-American mother airs the view of transracial adoption critics, who argue that the Caucasian family would struggle to help Isaiah develop his racial identity. On the other side, the adoptive family's attorney makes the case that Isaiah's need for a safe home, quality education, and good medical care should outweigh racial considerations. Although the film ends in typical Hollywood fashion, with the boy's birth mother (Halle Berry) embracing the social worker who has lost custody of Isaiah, the reality is often much stickier.

Research and professional opinion has been divided on the subject. Proponents of transracial adoption argue that the opportunity for a loving and caring home often alleviates racial barriers and fulfills the child's immediate needs for safety and security. Critics of transracial adoption oppose such practice on the grounds that it detaches the minority child from his or her culture. They claim, perhaps rightly, that white adoptive parents are less prepared to handle the challenges minority children face as a result of prejudice and persecution from the dominant culture.

My own view is that the immediacy of the child's need for a permanent, secure family attachment is more important than any underlying racial considerations, particularly for children already in the child welfare system. The truth is that many of these children already are being raised in homes in which the foster parent is not the same race as the child. Providing permanent, secure family relations is invaluable, and with reasonable effort adoptive parents can become versed in the customs and traditions of their child's culture of origin.

As for my own family, while we are still learning and adjusting to our cultural differences and will continue to do so, our experience testifies to the fact that transracial families can work. My wife is half Mexican American and half Caucasian. Five of my six children are part Mexican American and part Caucasian (there is some uncertainty in the exact proportions, but that sometimes happens with adoption; one has to learn to live with ambiguity). One of my sons is part Guatemalan and part Caucasian. Some may argue we are not a genuine transracial adoptive family because my wife and children share a Hispanic heritage, but I would argue we are—partially because of a transracial marriage, partially because all of my children *are* biracial, and partially because I am a different ethnicity than my children. Around six years of age, when my Guatemalan son began to discover his adoptive and ethnic distinctiveness, we spent time reading and discussing Guatemala, looking at pictures of people from Guatemala, and studying the countries of Central America on the globe. We tried to help him understand what Guatemala and being part Guatemalan meant to him. When Nathan was almost eight he read an article in a church magazine[6] that made a major impact on his life. The article described an eleven-year-old little boy in Guatemala named Jairo. Perhaps just as important as the story's characterization of the child, were the depictions of the green surroundings of Guatemala, the ancient Mayan ruins where the boy liked to visit, and what it was like for Jairo to attend church in his small town. It helped Nathan to see what daily life was like for that little boy, to appreciate some of the similarities and differences in their lives. Of course around that same time his teacher at church told us that he had told her he was from "guacamole." Clearly, we had more work to do. But now at the age of thirteen, he seems comfortable with himself and proud of his ethnicity. Will the issue arise again? Absolutely. But we are doing the best we can to help him understand his ethnic culture and heritage.

In addition to expanding his cultural awareness, I would argue that the adoption experience has given Nathan what the early sociologist Max Weber calls "life chances."* These life chances: the social, emotional, educational, and spiritual opportunities afforded to a child through adoption—must certainly be factored in alongside racial and ethnic identity issues, if we wish to obtain a successful adoption outcome. When I think of what Nathan's life might have been like had his birth mother not immigrated to the U.S. while pregnant with Nathan but had remained in Guatemala, I can't help but conclude how grateful I am that he's here with us as a part of our family. I am confident we can help him stay connected to his culture and develop his ethnic identity while providing the safety, security, and attachment he would have otherwise lacked. Children need a permanent home and his birth family was not able to provide that for him under their conditions, however she had the foresight to allow him to be adopted and have the opportunities in life he now enjoys.

---

* Max Weber's concept of life chances will be discussed further later in the book. Essentially, he argued that complex factors such as a family's upbringing determine what chances a person has at upward social mobility and other measures of fulfillment.

The Open-Adoption Continuum

A relatively recent trend, *open adoption,* refers to personal contact between birth family members, adoptive parents, and the adoptive child. Contact can come in the form of letters, e-mail, one-time information-sharing, or ongoing personal visits. Although adoption-speak typically distinguishes between open and closed adoptions on an either/or basis—where closed adoption does not involve correspondences or personal contact—it is more appropriate to describe open adoption along a continuum.[7] At one end is a completely closed adoption in which there is never any contact between the birth and adoptive families. A little further along, we find a onetime letter from the birth family, usually the birth mother, to the adopted parents and child. Typically, the letter explains the birth parent's decisions about adoptive placement and is answered, via the agency, by a letter of reassurance from the adoptive parents. Still further, we find a onetime personal visit in which the parents get to know each other on a first name basis at the time of placement. Although this allows the two parties to meet, feel comfortable with one another, and ask questions of each other, it limits their ability to communicate in the years to come. There may be a periodic exchange of letters and pictures under the supervision of the adoption agency or facilitator but no long-term personal contact.

When face-to-face meetings take place on a somewhat regular basis we begin to see what professionals describe as an open adoption. At first adoptive families and birth family members may agree to allow annual or periodic visits at a park or other neutral location. Later, as they become more comfortable, they may have special holiday and birthday visits in the adoptive family's home. Among some of the most open adoptive families, we may even find the birth mother or other birth family members making frequent social visits, as if they were family friends, welcome at any time. At the far end are cases where the birth mother may live with the adoptive family for a short period of time, either in a transitional stage, or until she is able to care for herself and move forward in her life.

One of the main advantages of open adoption is that it allows the child to acquire knowledge about his birth family while growing up. Why is this a good thing? Because it limits the child's chances of developing romanticized notions about his biologic parents and clears up some of the confusion surrounding the child's identity. The child who instead grows up in a closed adoption may have fantastic notions about his birth parents, envisioning them as flawless heroes, foils to his "mean" or "ogre-like" adoptive parents. This is particularly true when the child is being disciplined. Children in open adoptions, on the other hand, generally have clear and realistic expectations; they understand that the parent can't always be the good guy.

Sometimes, however, acquaintance with the birth parents can be extremely disheartening for a child. There is no guarantee as to the judgment and intentions of the birth parents and when the parent has ongoing problems—be they issues of mental health, substance abuse, legal wrongdoing, or other more generalized personal problems—open adoption may cause these problems to bubble to the surface. When a "flaky" birth parent exits, enters, exits, re-enters, and exits their adopted child's life, it is the child who will bear the repercussions. Parents considering open adoption should take preemptive measures. It is very important to have a plan that includes clearly spelled-out boundaries and roles, the ultimate say in whether or not the open relationship is beneficial to the child, and the ability to limit visitation or terminate the open adoption should the birth parent become harmful to the child or make attempts to undermine the adoptive parents' authority.

Special-Needs Children

In the language of adoption, special needs is a catchall term used to describe a variety of concerns or difficulties a child may have: medical problems, disabilities, behavioral or emotional problems, histories of abuse, neglect or abandonment, or prenatal drug exposure. It can also refer to difficult-to-place children who are of a minority race or who come in biological sibling groups. At times it may even refer to age, for when children reach a certain age—three years old in some states, five years old in others—they can be harder to place in adoptive homes. In some circumstances, the term special needs can be applied to children who presently do not have health or behavioral problems but who are nonetheless considered "at risk" because of their socio-emotional histories or genetic predisposition to such problems. For instance, if the birth mother has a mental illness that is partially derived from genetic causes, such as depression or schizophrenia, the child may be considered to have special needs by virtue of his or her elevated risk of developing these mental illnesses.

Prospective parents must be willing to accept that special-needs adopted children may require extra visits to the doctor, therapeutic support, and extensive services and intervention. While agencies and community supports hopefully will assist the adoptive families in this work, adopting a special-needs child takes a rare kind of person. Many adoptive parents describe a feeling of divine purpose, meaning, or calling as they perform this labor of love in their homes.

Older-Age Adoptions

Adopting children at older ages, usually age three years old and older, is becoming more and more common. The phrase *age of placement* is used to describe the age when the child is first placed in the home. Age of placement is more useful to researchers as a means of evaluating and predicting a child's emotional behavior than the age when an adoption is legally finalized, since legal processes may creep along, taking anywhere from a few months to several years to complete. Tellingly, a child placed in the home early in her infancy, but unable to have her adoption finalized until age three, will have a more promising emotional and behavioral outlook than a three-year-old placed in a home immediately prior to when her adoption is finalized. A tremendous amount of human development occurs in the first three years of life, and each successive month that a child is waiting for a permanent adoptive placement further hinders her growth and development. That is why age of placement is so important.

In a later chapter, I will discuss the outcomes of children adopted at older ages, but I want to point out, here, that there is great diversity in older adoptions, both in their arrangement and chances for long-term success. Commonly adoptions of older children are handled through Child Protective Services or international adoption agencies, but they can happen within almost any adoptive agency. Few older-age adoptions are simple. When compared with children who are adopted before the age of three, older children tend to show lower social, emotional, and behavioral outcomes. The older adopted child has usually had some history of abuse, neglect, or trauma and is often designated as having special needs. Prospective couples who wish to adopt an older child are advised to seek out additional medical and therapeutic support as soon as possible.

Family Composition

As has long been the case, marriage is by far the statistical norm for adoptive parents. In the 2000 U.S. Census, 78 percent of all adoptive parents were heterosexually married couples.[8] However in recent years there has been a growing minority of other adoptive family forms. Single parent adoptions take place mostly in female-headed households, and the tendency is for these parents to adopt older-aged children rather than infants.[9] In 1993, it was estimated that single parents were responsible for about 8 percent of all adoptions, and that number has been steadily rising. In 2002, the percentage of single, female-headed homes adopting from the public foster care system was 31 percent.[10]

Family composition, of course, does not only refer to the marital status of the adoptive parents. With adoptive families, family composition may refer to whether or not the adopted children come from biological sibling groups and to how well these children relate to other members of the family. Adoptive families who adopt one child at a time, if they adopt more than once, will likely adopt from different birth families. It can be difficult to manage relations with two different sets of birth parents, each with their own history, culture, and set of values. So when making choices about family composition, prospective parents should consider their willingness to adopt biological sibling groups.

Still, adopting biological sibling groups is not always easy. Couples may feel overwhelmed to find multiple children of differing ages entering their home all at once. Moreover, children with a shared family history do not necessarily respond similarly to their new adoptive parents. If an older child is used to taking a caregiving or parenting role—marriage and family therapists call this a *parentified child*—that child may find it hard to allow the adoptive parents to care for her younger siblings. When we adopted a sibling set, our elder daughter really struggled when I would help our younger boy get a drink of water or take him to the bathroom to change his diaper. In an attempt to stop me, she would run up from behind and try to push me out of the way, loudly protesting, "I do it." We had to set firm boundaries and meet her needs for nurturing before she trusted us enough to allow us to care for her younger brother.

Biological sibling group adoption can be particularly challenging when a family already has children in the home, because the introduction of a new sibling group can disrupt the existing birth order, shifting the power dynamics established in the household. When these sorts of struggles occur in my clinical work, I often recommend Theraplay techniques to enhance attachment. But, even with therapy, adjusting to a new set of children who are biologically related and already have an existing sibling dynamic requires patience and emotional strength.

One of the keys to managing the inclusion of newly adopted children into the home is to openly acknowledge their differences.[10] In therapy sessions with adoptive families who have a mix of adopted and biological children, I use an allegorical puppet story about a frog adopted by a family of bunnies. In the story hopping can symbolize many things—play, work, temperament, race, etc.—though what the hopping signifies is less important than the underlining theme; namely, that accommodating a child from another family is challenging and requires a degree of acceptance, for all animals "hop" in their own way. Families have distinct rules, values, and approaches to discipline, and we have to acknowledge and respect differences, rather than force compliance, co-optation, or assimilation.

Summary

The notion of diversity enters into multiple facets of the adoptive family's life. Diversity means more than simply the ethnic background or race of the family members. Rather it encompasses the full range of choices an adoptive family makes about how to live their life. Hopefully, the discussion of transracial adoptions, open adoptions, special-needs and older-age adoptions, and biological sibling group adoptions has provided you with a basic introduction into the vastly different kinds of adoptive family forms that exist today. Recognizing these differences is the first step toward understanding what kinds of adoptive choices are right for your family.

Chapter Four
How Well Do Adoptive Children Fare?

On April 10, 2010, when Torry Hansen of Shelbyville, Tennessee, sent Russian seven-year-old, Artyem Saviliev, on an unaccompanied United Airlines flight from Washington, D.C., to Moscow, she left a note inside the boy's pocket that described her adopted son as "mentally unstable," with "severe psychopathic issues."[1] The note went on to say, "I was lied to and misled by the Russian orphanage workers and director regarding his mental stability and other issues." Although the boy's flight and the international politics surrounding it are exceptional, his difficult behavior and the mystery of its origin constitute a legitimate concern. Many children, both domestically and internationally, have complex medical and environmental histories including fetal alcohol syndrome, drug exposure, and experiences of abuse and neglect that require extensive medical and psychological support. As you read this chapter, you may well be asking yourself, "If I'm going to adopt a child, what's the likelihood things will work out?" This is a fairly complicated issue because no two adoptions are alike, although the research shows that most adoptions work out successfully.

There are two main camps concerning adoption outcomes. According to the "adoption deficit camp," adoption outcomes are generally poor. Members of this group note the higher proportion of adopted children receiving therapy and the cognitive and emotional deficits the children have due to histories of abuse and neglect. They also point to increasing numbers of adopted children seeking reunion with their birth family in adulthood, viewing this as a sign the adopted family has failed in some way. At one point there was a failed movement among this group to coin a psychiatric disorder, Adopted Child Syndrome, although this has never gained acceptance in the professional community.[2] The most prominent proponents of this view are David Kirchner, a psychologist in private practice in Woodbury, New York, and the author of *Adoption: Unchartered Waters,* and Nancy Verrier, a marriage and family therapist in private practice in Lafayette, California, most famous for her self-published book *The Primal Wound: Understanding the Adopted Child.*[3]

Those in the second camp, this author included, argue that adopted children are generally raised in homes that are more favorable in several dimensions than those of their birth families. Adoptive families use a disproportionate amount of therapeutic services, they claim, not because of the insidious nature of the adoption process, but because of the adoptive parents' socio-economic status, education levels, and comfort with therapy. According to this latter group, adopted children have favorable outcomes in several dimensions and are generally far better off than children who remain in foster care or with unfit birth families. Notable in this camp are Brent Miller, a professor of human and family development at the Utah State University, Harold Grotevant, a professor emeritus at the University of Minnesota, and Marinus Van IJzendoorn, the chair of the Department of Education and Child Studies at Leiden University in the Netherlands.

Both camps have interesting arguments, but adoption experiences are complex and distinctive and must be understood on a case-by-case basis. This is part of what led me to write this book. As I began to work clinically with adoptive families, I recognized that how adoptive families *do* adoption differs, and the variance in how they *do* adoption may lead to different clinical treatment needs. Some may be struggling with attachment issues. Others may have identity concerns because of the open or closed nature of their adoption, because the adoption is transracial, or because the family has chosen not to publicly disclose the adoption in their social network. Moreover, the kinds of choices adoptive families make about how to manage adoption-related family issues may affect the kinds of clinical needs that arise. That is why when I meet with adoptive families, one of the first questions I ask is "How do you *do* adoption in your family?" I want to acknowledge that their adoptive family experiences and their choices about how to handle adoption-related family matters will be different from those of my own family and from other adoptive families I have counseled. Valuing a family's unique adoption narrative helps me understand how to best support them.

Resisting the Deficit View of Adoption

One other precautionary note is necessary before we delve into the research related to adopted child outcomes. That is, we need to exercise sound judgment in "resisting the deficit view of adoption."[4] In a recent article about the benefits of adoption, Patricia Gorman, an associate professor at Saint Joseph College in West Hartford, Connecticut, points out that many social workers view adoption as a second-best alternative. This view is psychologically damaging to adoptive parents, Gorman claims, who languish over their infertility and regard it as a personal flaw. Clinicians and adoptive parents must resist the socially constructed notion that adopted families are doomed to "incipient pathology, life time deficiency, diminished status, and problematic futures,"[5] in order to optimize the family's chances for adoptive success.

Perhaps some social workers, therapists, and clinicians who work with adoptive families hold onto the deficit perspective because they only see one side of the equation—a clinical population of adoptive families. On the basis of their experiences with adoptive families in therapy, they begin to extrapolate to adoptive families in general. That leads to misguided conclusions. As this chapter will review, the research literature in the general population has found that most adopted children have satisfactory outcomes when assessed by parental self-reports.[6]

So while it is true that adoptive families are more likely to seek therapy,[7] this probably has more to do with the characteristic features of the adoptive parent population than with the children's behaviors. In a meta-analysis of the research literature presented to the American Association for Marriage and Family Therapy National Conference in Austin, Texas, in 2006,[8] I reported that adoptive parents have a higher average level of education, income, and familiarity with therapists and social workers than parents in the general population because they are more willing to participate in therapy.

In addition, it appears that for some families there may be a developmental disjuncture between the individual and family's life cycle when the adopted child reaches the teenage years. At a time when adoptive parents feel they've already discussed everything there is to discuss about adoption with their child, teens are beginning their identity development in earnest and raising new questions about adoption issues. This is also the time when many adoptive families seek out therapeutic services. Typically, as adoptive parents adjust to meet their child's needs, the family system returns to a sense of balance or homeostasis. While some adopted children clearly have a need for therapy because of their histories and special needs, in many cases the emotional and behavioral problems we find in adolescents are rooted in unresolved identity issues.

As for their spousal relationships, many adoptive couples experience improved marital satisfaction upon making the transition to parenthood.[9] This is in direct contrast to biological parents who show a dip in marital contentment after having their first child.[10] Moreover, research shows that adoptive parents have lower divorce rates than parents in biologically constructed families and that adoptive fathers tend to be more active in the parenting role.[11]

Equally encouraging are reports revealing that parents generally are pleased with the adoption experience and able to develop close relationships with their children. In one of the most conclusive adoption outcome studies to date, Peter Benson and his research team at the Search Institute in Minneapolis, Minnesota, found that adoptive parents who adopted infants reported "excellent" attachment with their children; in addition, a seminal study conducted in 1988 examined parents' attitudes toward their adopted children and reported an impressive 84 percent satisfaction rate.[12]

While both of these studies focused on infant adoptions, it has been shown consistently that adoption experiences turn out well at all ages. James Rosenthal, a professor at the School of Social Work at Oklahoma University, found that although the percentage of adoptions that disrupt or dissolve increases from about 2 percent for infant adoptions to 10–15 percent for older, special-needs adoptions, parental satisfaction with older, special-needs adoptions remained high at 75 precent.[13] On top of that, two adoption outcome studies stemming from Nicole Jaffari-Bimmel's work as a postdoctoral student under Van IJsendoorn at Leiden University suggest that adoption can be a "protective factor," improving the lives of children whose alternative options for care would have been undesirable.[14]

> "Adoption may even be considered a protective factor"[15] because when adopted children are compared with illegitimate children who were institutionalized, remained with their mothers, or who were later returned to their mothers, adopted children fared far better, especially those in two-parent families.[16]

Finally, in 2005, a comprehensive study concerning adoption outcomes by Steven Nickman, a psychiatrist at Massachusetts General Hospital and a clinical faculty member of the Harvard University Medical School, found that, in general, outcomes for adopted children were positive.[17] On the basis of the findings, Nickman suggests that adoption experiences vary widely, but when problems do occur they are less a result of the adoption itself than preexisting conditions. From a therapeutic standpoint, Nickman's study has important implications beyond just presenting a favorable picture of adoption outcomes. The study suggests that adoption methods and adoptive families can be categorized into subgroups, so clinicians will have a better idea of how particular types of adoption affect outcomes. For instance, when problems occur in infant, international, and transracial adoptions, treatment is often needed for identity formation issues, whereas with older adoptions we need to pay attention to developmental delays, attachment disturbances, and posttraumatic stress disorder (PTSD).

Taken together, these outcome findings should give you reason for hope. Trust that whatever issues do arise in the adoption can be dealt with given sufficient knowledge of the child's medical and personal history. Remember that detailed information about an adopted child's past will yield useful information for a clinician to utilize in therapy and should always be a first priority. But for a better explanation of the specific historical factors I'm referring to, let's move on to the seven adoption outcome factors (Figure 4.1) that form the core of this book: (1) age of placement, (2) placement history (including attachment patterns), (3) medical/special needs, (4) parental care history, (5) prenatal/neonatal care history, (6) demographic variables, and (7) developmental issues. In my work as a marriage and family therapist, I have found that these seven factors tend to determine the level of difficulty parents will have with an adoption. Challenging adoptions should not necessarily be avoided, but they may require extra services, more parental effort, and additional support from extended family and parents' social support systems.

---

1. Age of Placement
2. Placement History (including attachment patterns)
3. Medical/Special Needs
4. Parental Care History (including physical or sexual abuse, neglect, and abandonment)
5. Prenatal/Neonatal History
6. Demographic Variables (race, socio-economic status, educational opportunities—what the German sociologist Max Weber called "life chances")
7. Developmental Issues

FIGURE 4.1 Seven factors salient to adoption outcomes

It should be pointed out that although these seven factors appear to make a difference in how hard adoptive families will have to work to ensure a successful adoption outcome, they do not mean a child is doomed. Even in rare scenarios in which a couple adopts a child with several adoptive risk factors—i.e., the child is older, the child displays developmental delays, the child has been abused and occupied several foster homes— there is still a great opportunity for success. It simply means there will be additional challenges to overcome and the family may need extra support services. But you should be realistic. Before starting your adoptive search, you may have to redefine what a "successful outcome" means, given your particular set of circumstances.

Informed adoptive parents begin with the end in mind. They seek out a medical and developmental prognosis and gather information about the child's mental ability, age, and parental history. They make a decision on the basis of whether

or not they can raise the child to maturity, and their predic-
tion of how close the parent-child relationship will remain
over time. Informed adoptive parents generally want to know
about the child's cognitive capacity. They want to have faith
that their child will do well in school, be happy in a career that
is fulfilling, and eventually become an intelligent contributor
to the world around them. Understandably, most prospective
adoptive parents also hope that the child will grow up to be
physically healthy, free from sickness and medical concerns,
and capable of living to maturity and beginning a family of
their own. Because hope for a positive adoption outcome is a
near-universal concern, the seven factors that appear to affect
those outcomes the most will be addressed in the chapters that
follow.

Summary
Occasionally adopted children have significant medical needs,
behavioral problems, or other challenges that leave adopted
parents worried about the future outcome of their children.
Thoughts such as, "Will my child ever overcome his propensity
to misbehave?" "How is she going to ever go to college when
she has such serious cognitive deficits?" or, "Will she always
struggle with not trusting the people who care about her?" are
understandably troubling. However, keep in mind that parents
of biological children have many of the same worries. One of
the most remarkable facts presented in this chapter is that 84
percent of adoptive parents reported being satisfied with their
adopted child's outcome—a remarkably high percentage. Despite the rare, but true, examples of poor adoption outcomes
such as that of Russian seven-year-old Artyem Saviliev, most
adoptions fare very well. The odds are in your favor if you are
aware of the kind of adoption experience you are seeking and
take advantage of the support services (often professional services) available to adoptive families. Too often adoptions fail

because prospective couples don't really understand what to expect, nor how to treat behavioral and mental health issues as they arise. The remainder of this book is devoted to seven salient factors affecting adoption outcomes. Knowing what these factors are and understanding what they may mean to your adoptive search will help you and your family make the right choices when selecting a method of adoption.

Chapter Five
Age of Placement, Placement History, and Attachment

Age of placement is a significant predictor of outcome for an adopted child, and you will need to consider carefully what ages of children you would be prepared and willing to adopt. Adoptions at all ages have good outcomes, but infant adoptions have the highest rate of success. Several researchers have documented that infant adoptions (out of all adoptions) most frequently result in good parent-child attachments and lead to satisfying relationships when the adopted child reaches adulthood.[1] But keep in mind that infant adoptions are not without their obstacles. They often are associated with long waiting periods prior to placement and can be very expensive due to the high demand for infants in the adoption market. If you want children in the near future (weeks to months after clearing the background check and training as opposed to many months or years) or if you cannot afford the costs associated with infant adoption, you may wish to consider adopting an older child.

Many couples considering adoption picture a newborn or young infant when they first imagine their new family. It may take some time and emotional reckoning to change that vision into the reality of adopting an older child, particularly if that child possesses less desirable traits as a result of his life history. Older children are more likely to have histories of traumatic, abusive, or otherwise pathogenic care when compared with infants, and this environmental history often brings with it emotional and behavioral problems. As a parent of four infant adoptions and two adoptions of older-aged children, I'll admit the clinical problems arising in older children are generally more difficult to address than those in infants.

Yet older adoptions have their rewards. The resilience of older children is inspiring, and I'm routinely left in awe of children's ability to overcome the traumatic experiences they have encountered early on in life. Having lived through multiple home placements or troubled stays in foster care, many develop an appreciation for a loving family, a good home, and secure relationships that younger adopted children may take for granted. Another benefit of older children is that most have readily apparent needs. There is a certain gratification in giving a child a life opportunity he did not have coming from a background of poverty or deprivation.

More than two decades ago, Marriane Berry and Richard Barth conducted one of the most comprehensive studies of clinical issues associated with the adoption of older-aged children.[2] At the time Berry served as a research assistant to Dr. Barth, who was an associate professor at the School of Social Welfare at the University of California at Berkeley. The two examined 927 older adoptions from 1980 to 1984 and found that children with histories of abuse or neglect adopted at age 3 or older were significantly more likely to have behavioral problems. These problems varied widely and included lying; stealing; hurting themselves or others through physical violence; whining; withdrawing; food hoarding; lashing out; and sexually acting out. Not surprisingly, the research team determined that adopted children with aggressive, hyperactive, and antisocial behavioral problems had a "greater risk of adoption instability."[3] More interesting was the researchers' hypothesis that behavior problems were more common in older adopted children due to the resentment some of these children feel when adoption means disconnecting from the birth family. Although these behaviors are treatable with time and therapy, it is vital that the home environment involves patient parents and siblings who will provide structure, engagement, and nurturing to strengthen the child's attachment to the family.

In fact it is widely believed that the *family system* is the most critical element for healing older children with attachment and behavioral issues. Marriage and family therapists hold to a theoretical view called *systems theory*, which understands the family as an interconnected set of relationships through which circular or recursive interactions cause typical patterns to form. These patterns guide personal and familial behaviors, thoughts, and feelings. However, when we talk about adoption, things get tricky. Adding just one adopted child to the family can transform the relationships of the adoptive nuclear family, birth family, and extended family, as well as the social networks of both the adoptive and birth families. For our purposes, the main point is that family systems inform the treatment concerns of older adopted children with emotional, behavioral, and other special needs, and it is good practice to consult a marriage and family therapist who can help you navigate the interpersonal changes that occur within and across families when adopting an older child.

At all ages the transition the child makes from one set of adults to another is critical. For successful attachment, infants need affection and nurturing from the earliest stages of the adoption. Reciprocal and attentive cooing, soft talking, play—all are important in strengthening the bond between an adoptive parent and child. Infants can feel disruption if they have had time to develop a connection with their birth parents, so that displacement from these former caregivers means an abrupt shift in the source of parental affection. Sometimes this transition can be even harder for older children who have lived with birth families for many months or years. When possible,

I recommend transitional visits to help ease the transfer of the child's attachments.

One good model of transitional care can be found in the Foster Care Support Foundation, a volunteer-led, non-profit organization, in Roswell, Georgia, that provides clothing, toys, and equipment to foster children throughout Georgia. Below are the foundation's guidelines for home transition.[4] They represent those across the United States and are a good glimpse of the way healthy attachment is fostered through gradual increase in the foster child's exposure to the adoptive family.

1. Preparation—Begin talking with the child about the im pending move.
2. First Meeting—2 to 3 hour meeting with foster parents, adoptive family, and child/children preferably in the foster home.
3. Outside Home Visits—Two or three, 3 to 4 hour visits outside the home (e.g., at a park or fast food restaurant) within 1 to 3 days of each other.
4. Visiting the New Home—A minimum of three 4 to 6 hour day visits with just the adoptive family and child (first visit introduced by the foster parent).
5. Overnight Visits—4 to 6 overnight visits in the new home.

In practice, most transitional visits go well. After seeing how the family relates to the child, the social worker feels comfortable making a placement that allows for healthy attachment. Unfortunately, these visits do not always happen. Clinically, I have dealt with many children whose social workers gave no thought or concern for their move to a new placement. Transitional visits were not made, and hasty placements robbed the adoptive family of the opportunity to learn how to relate to the new child. If you are adopting a child through the child welfare system, be sure to inquire after transitional visits, for doing so may have an enormous impact on the long-term relationship you have with your child.

Our youngest son, Danny, was cared for by a wonderful set of foster parents, a retired couple who specialize in caring for infants until an adoptive family can be found, typically two to three months after foster placement. Never mind my PhD and years of practice, what I learned from this couple was invaluable. They taught me how Danny liked to be put to sleep, what exercises he had been doing to stimulate his growth—personal attributes and affections that no research could have explained. Their advice made the transfer of attachment so much smoother. We learned how Danny liked to be cared for and how to make him comfortable in our home.

When it comes to older adoptions, I cannot overstate the importance of first impressions. In earlier research (as well as research by other scholars), I've found that behavioral patterns established immediately following the time of placement are defining predictors of the success of the long-term relationship.[5] Children often engage in "homeostatic testing," to test their adoptive parents' limits, and the parental response to this testing is critical. Elsewhere I discuss how most children will go through predictable periods of testing the new parent-child relationship:

> After being placed in a new home, there was almost always a honeymoon period where the child was likable and well behaved. That honeymoon may have lasted a couple of hours or a few weeks, but after the honeymoon phase the testing would begin. A child would misbehave in some way to test the limits to see how the foster parents would respond. Reminiscent of Bowlby's protest phase,[6] the child felt a need to "see how far they could go" to test the limits of security in the relationship. If the foster parent remained consistent, understood and respected the child's need for testing the new relationship, but did not react negatively nor participate in the emotionally charged situation, the foster child would begin to

open themselves for attachment once the foster parents "passed the test." There would be new phases of honeymoon and testing, but the future tests would diminish in their intensity over time. If the foster parent responded in an emotionally reactive manner to the homeostatic test, the foster child closed himself off, the tests and misbehaviors would escalate, and attachment efforts were hampered. It became critical, in Bowenian fashion, to help foster parents respond positively and proactively, rather than reactively to their attachment-impaired youth.[7]

The key for adoptive and foster parents is not to react or participate in emotionally charged situations. That is so easy to say and so hard to do—but it is the key. Most displays of insubordination, disrespect, and antisocial behavior are tests to see how the parents will respond. If parents' behavioral responses are calm and loving, no matter what the provocation, the child will eventually learn to trust the parents and the child's behaviors will calm down.

Environmental Trauma and Older-Age Adoption

Frequently, I hear the phrase "older special-needs adoptions," applied liberally as if all older children have special needs. Special needs and age of placement are not always one and the same. Older children may qualify as having special needs simply on the basis of their age. On the other hand, medical problems; prenatal exposure to harmful substances; histories of abuse, neglect, or abandonment; and other factors may designate a child as "special needs," regardless of age.

As I've said, older children in the adoption pool generally have had to endure adverse and traumatic experiences in their early years. These experiences may contribute to their behavior problems and in some cases cause existing special needs to become apparent. For example, it is common for children previously in foster care to have undergone multiple placements. The research is clear that increased multiple placements hurt the children's sense of attachment and security and may result in emotional and behavioral complications.[8] At the same time, when adopted children have resided in orphanages, particularly those outside the United States, the children may appear and act younger than their age: stunted development is a common correlate to the orphanage experience.

One of the starkest examples of how a child's environment can influence their growth and development was brought to my attention at an adoption symposium in Utah in 2003. A medical doctor from Minnesota, who specializes in caring for children in Eastern European orphanages, showed pictures of a boy who appeared to be eight or nine years old. This doctor reported that the boy's chronological age was seventeen years old. It soon became apparent to me (and is substantiated in several studies)[9] that a child's early experiences not only affected him emotionally and behaviorally but had long-lasting physical and cognitive implications, as well.

The circumstances of most domestic older adoptions are not that extreme. The foster care system in the United States does an adequate job of ensuring the majority of children get basic nutrition, nurturing touch, and periodic monitoring by social workers. Even where physical or developmental difficulties exist, most parents find adoption of older-age children rewarding. They simply may require additional clinical and therapeutic support.

Placement History

To conduct a realistic assessment of a child's background and decide whether you are ready to adopt, it is important to understand a child's placement history. Studies indicate that multiple placements are detrimental to a child's sense of attachment to parental figures, and may lead to increased risk for emotional and behavioral disturbances.[10] In *Family Therapy Magazine,* I write:

For children and adolescents who have had little constancy in their life, providing consistency in relationships is critical in building trust and attachment. When youth have historically had years of instability and insecurity-provoking upheaval, they need relational consistency before they will begin to open themselves up emotionally to make connections, attachments, and trusting relationships. Initially, attachment-impaired youth have a difficult time trusting or relying upon their new foster or adoptive parent. In fact they will often try to maladaptively handle dilemmas on their own and seek to push others from their lives. As [marriage and family therapists] help parents to consistently listen and communicate with their child, remain available without becoming intrusive or overbearing, and patiently allow the child to gradually attach at the child's own pace, the facilitation of connection will occur. Consistency also means permanency. Having a stable, long-term sense of permanency in family relationships ensures that the child has a consistent set of "family rules" to live by and family relationships with whom to root or secure one's self. Along with love and support, time and familiarity with healthy family environments provides an added measure of stability and security necessary for attachment-building.[11]

All of this is why appropriate disclosure of information and proper preparation for a placement *before* the placement occurs is so important in permanency planning. Children removed from their biological homes need to be placed in prospective adoptive homes where there is great likelihood that adoption will occur without disruption. By the second placement after removal, children should have a permanent home—beyond that, serious problems may begin to arise. Of course, all of this also underscores why we need more available adoptive homes.

Attachment and Reactive Attachment Disorder (RAD)

Sometimes needy children, especially those who are older and have had multiple placements, will not respond readily to expressions of affection from adoptive parents. A former student of mine aptly described this non-responsiveness in the title for her thesis, *How to Hug a Rock*.[12] Children with such attachment

issues may have ambivalent feelings about their new family, or
they may simply not know how to respond. In fact, many older
children adopted from U.S. foster care systems are commonly
diagnosed with *reactive attachment disorder (RAD)*.

One of the early researchers of child development, Erik
Erikson, suggested that the first year of a child's life centers
around his development of trust or mistrust in parents or caregivers.[13] If an infant is loved, cared for, shown tenderness, fed,
and consistently fulfilled in the requirements of basic needs,
that child will grow to trust his parents. A few years later another noted researcher, John Bowlby, produced *Attachment
and Loss,* a definitive, three-volume compendium on the subject of attachment;[14] and, from there, Mary Salter Ainsworth,
who studied under Bowlby at the Tavistock Clinic in London,
ascribed practical application strategies to attachment theory.
In *Patterns of Attachment,*[15] Ainsworth develops an interesting test by which attachment patterns may be discerned. The
so-called "Strange Situation" involves a twenty-minute play
period during which parents enter a room with their child, allow the child to play freely with the variety of toys according to
the child's choosing, and then inconspicuously leave the room
while strangers are present. On the basis of children's reactions
to these strangers, the researchers can determine patterns of
attachment.

Not surprisingly, what researchers have discovered is that
children who get their needs met feel secure. When a baby
cries, parents should feed him, change his diaper, or otherwise
meet the child's needs. Until the child is older and can soothe
himself, parents should help to regulate the infant's emotions
by balancing key dimensions of care that foster attachment.[16]

In recent years, we have learned a lot about how to help
attachment-impaired children through Theraplay. Developed
by Ann Jernberg, in Chicago, in the late 1960s and early 1970s,
Theraplay is a form of interactive bonding that balances the

four dimensions of healthy attachments—structure, engagement, nurture, and challenge—in the parent-child relationship. Today, it is one of the most compelling therapeutic models for treating adoptive and foster children with attachment concerns. From Bowlby, Ainsworth, and the work of the Theraplay Institute, we have learned that if parents and their children engage in relational patterns that balance love, structure, care, and support, then secure attachments will develop.

However, when a child's primary caregiver is inconsistent—sometimes providing appropriate care but often neglecting to do so—the child may develop a pattern of *anxious/ambivalent attachment*. The result is that the child anxiously wants love and attention but reacts with ambivalence once given that attention. Adults who have developed an anxious/ambivalent attachment pattern while growing up describe a feeling of "waiting for the other shoe to drop," expecting that something bad will happen whenever love is expressed toward them. Among younger children, Ainsworth has suggested cases of anxious/ambivalent attachment are apparent in two ways: children who become anxious around strangers even when their mother is present; and children who become upset when the mother leaves, and then express ambivalence when she returns.[17]

When the parent or primary caregiver is consistent, but consistently bad in their care, the child will develop a pattern of *anxious/avoidant attachment*. This is commonly observed in adoptions in which a child was formerly abused, neglected, or both. To the extent that caregivers are consistently hurtful, the young child learns to avoid and ignore people, mistrusting their intentions. She comes to learn that every birthday party will soon be spoiled by a drunken, angry, or embarrassing parent; that her parents won't pick her up from school, or that she'll have to walk home in the rain, even though her parents promised to be waiting in the school parking lot. While the experiences of children with anxious/avoidant attachment pattern are truly some of the saddest and most debilitating, therapy does provide reason for hope. When these children are adopted and the family attends family therapy sessions such as Theraplay, I have seen children turn their lives around. Most children want to feel secure in their family relationships, and play-based therapy may give children who have been abused and/or neglected confidence in the intentions of their new parents.

One final behavior pattern that has emerged in the literature of attachment theory is known as *disorganized attachment*. Children who exhibit disorganized attachment have no clear, consistent pattern of attachment and may exhibit all three patterns at different times, occasionally showing preference for one pattern over the others. Once again, alternating poor and inconsistent care appears to lead to this pattern. Children with disorganized attachment patterns may exhibit behaviors such as cowering in fright, rocking, or freezing (e.g., staring, looking intently, freezing their body activities when spoken to or when asked a question) and may lack awareness as to appropriate boundaries.

The birth parent often plays a crucial role in the systemic creation of attachment problems, usually because of abuse and/or neglect that triggers the child's removal from the home and consequent placement into custody. Pathogenic care, the name given to care causing health problems or difficulties in the child's ability to bond to his parents, is the source of behavioral problems we sometimes see in foster children and among children adopted through public child welfare agencies. Unfortunately, foster and adopted parents who care for children with explosive, disruptive behaviors often fail to give attention to attachment issues at the root of the problem, thus exacerbating the issue rather than fixing it. Too often adoptive parents and children get stuck in a lockstep "dance," whereby each response to the other's behavior only works to perpetuate the cycle.

One of the most respected clinicians who has written about treatment for children with attachment issues is the clinical psychologist Daniel Hughes. Hughes has developed a type of attachment-based therapy called Dyadic Developmental Psychotherapy (DDP) and is the director of the DDP Institute in Williamsville, New York. As evident in his work with children on the East Coast—particularly foster and adoptive children, DDP is a useful model for treating children who have experienced trauma.

Hughes is the author of two very significant books regarding treatment for children with attachment disorders (*Facilitating Developmental Attachment* and *Attachment-Focused Family Therapy*)[18] in which he documents common symptoms of attachment-related behavioral problems. His findings are summarized in Figures 5.1 to 5.3.

- Poor response to discipline
- Aggressive or oppositional-defiant demeanor
- Interactions lacking mutual enjoyment and spontaneity
- Increased attachment, producing discomfort or resistance
- Poor planning/problem solving
- Ability to see only the extremes (all good/all bad)
- Pervasive shame
- Tendency to cling
- Poor eye contact
- Lying
- Food gorging
- Educational underachievement
- Refusal to participate in school
- Compulsion
- Social withdrawal

FIGURE 5.1 Symptoms of attachment-related behavior problems

As a researcher, Hughes theorizes that children's problematic behaviors stem from attachment problems and that to understand the root of these behaviors we have to delve "under the behavior"[20] to the feeling that provoked them. In Figure 5.2 you will find the underlying feelings Hughes has described previously in *Attachment-Focused Family Therapy*. This list is the most comprehensive and descriptive found in the literature and truly matches the experience of children I have seen clinically.

- Sense that only self can/will meet own needs
- Difficulty feeling safe
- Frequent sense of shame
- Sense of hopelessness and helplessness
- Fear of being vulnerable/dependent
- Fear of rejection
- Feeling of being "invisible"
- Inability to self-regulate intense affect – positive or negative
- Inability to engage in the co-regulation of affect – positive or negative
- Inability to be comforted when disciplined/hurt
- Inability to ask for help
- Felt sense that life is too hard
- Assumption that parents' motives/intentions are negative
- Lack of confidence in own abilities
- Lack of confidence that parents will comfort/assist during hard times
- Inability to understand why self does things
- Need to deny inner life because of overwhelming affect that exists there
- Inability to express inner life even if he or she wanted to
- Fear of failure
- Fear of trusting happiness
- Sense that discipline is harsh or unfair

FIGURE 5.2 children's feelings underlying attachment related behavior problems

Take a moment to familiarize yourself with these feelings, so that when disruptive behaviors surface you'll be able to recognize your children's needs and respond with appropriate empathy. According to Hughes, parents lacking attachment savvy may apply counterproductive strategies and consequences including, "chronic anger, harsh discipline, power struggles, not asking for help, not showing affection, difficulty sleeping, appetite problems, ignoring child, remaining isolated from child, reacting with rage and impulsiveness, lack of empathy for child, marital conflicts, withdrawal from relatives, anxiety and depression."[21] One should not automatically assume that these are "bad" parents. Just as children's behaviors are manifestations of more deeply rooted emotional discord, underneath these parental reactions lie complex, entirely justifiable feelings that have sparked the behaviors (see Figure 5.3 below).*

As an adoptive parent, the lesson is to focus on the feeling, not the behavior. To do otherwise is to risk an escalating cycle of misunderstandings that only widens the gulf between you and your child. In clinical theory, some suggest that working with children with these types of issues is best approached through *behaviorism*—a system whereby desirable behavior is rewarded and unwanted behavior is punished. For most children this approach works just fine. But for children with attachment disorders, I have found that behavior modification can exacerbate problems, for the child tends to personalize the punishment. Instead of thinking, "I shouldn't have done that because I don't like the consequences," a child with an attachment disorder will think, "They must really hate me; look how they punished me. Nobody who loves me would do that. I hate them, too." Children with attachment disorders often personalize consequences, which is why attachment-based play therapies such as Theraplay or DDP are so effective and why behavioral approaches tend to make things worse.

- Desire to help child develop well
- Love and commitment for child
- Desire to be a good parent
- Uncertainty about how to best meet child's needs
- Lack of confidence in ability to meet child's needs
- Specific failures with child associated with pervasive self-doubt
- Perceived lack of support and understanding from partner and other adults
- Difficulties addressing relationship problems with partner
- Felt sense that life is too hard
- Assumptions that child's motives/intentions are negative
- Pervasive sense of shame as a parent
- Conviction of helplessness and hopelessness
- Fear of being vulnerable/being hurt by child
- Fear of rejection by child
- Fear of failure as a parent
- Inability to understand why child does things
- Inability to understand why self reacts to child
- Tendency to associate child's functioning with aspects of own attachment history
- Belief that there is no other option besides the behavior tried

FIGURE 5.3 Parental feelings when raising children with attachment-related behavior problems

Clinical Diagnosis for Attachment Disorders

Although children present with a broad range of attachment disorders, RAD is currently the only diagnosis available in the American Psychiatric Association's *Diagnostic and Statistical Manual of Mental Disorders* (Revised 4th ed.). The *DSM-IV-TR* lists reactive attachment disorder (RAD) as an early childhood disorder.

Reactive attachment disorder is most commonly diagnosed in adopted and foster children who were abused and neglected in their infancy, toddler, and/or preschool years (though they may not be diagnosed until the early elementary school years depending on when they are removed from their biological family and placed in the child welfare system). Below are the criteria for RAD as they appear in *DSM-IV-TR*:[22]

- Markedly disturbed and developmentally inappropriate social-relatedness in most contexts
- Two types: inhibited, disinhibited
- Not a developmental delay, mental retardation, or pervasive developmental disorder
- Onset before age 5
- Pathogenic care (abuse or neglect)
- Presumption that pathogenic care is the cause of the behavior

Children with RAD will often have problems in their social relationships because attachment issues have stunted their capacity to relate to people. They will have problems with foster or adoptive parents, their friends, teachers, social workers, and almost anyone else they meet.

Most children with RAD will experience it in either its inhibited or disinhibited form, but not both. That dichotomous style is a key characteristic of RAD. A child who possesses an inhibited attachment style tends to avoid getting close to people, whereas a child with the disinihibited style is inclined to make superficial, indiscriminate attachments. In the *DSM-IV-TR,* an inhibited RAD pattern is described as

> persistent failure to initiate or respond in a developmentally appropriate way to most social interactions, as manifest by excessively inhibited, hypervigilant, or highly ambivalent, or contradictory responses, e.g. the child may respond to caregivers with a mixture of approach, avoidance and resistance to comforting, or may exhibit frozen watchfulness.[23]

Regarding a disinhibited RAD pattern, the *DSM-IV-TR* describes

> diffuse attachments as manifest by indiscriminate sociability with marked inability to exhibit appropriate selective attachments, e.g. excessive familiarity with relative strangers or lack of selectivity in choice of attachment figures.[24]

While inhibited RAD seems readily understandable given the abuse and/or neglect histories of the child (it seems logical that if people abuse you, you would want to avoid them), disinhibited RAD is harder to define. Allow an example from my doctoral internship at Rosemary's Children Services in Pasadena, CA, to illustrate:

> It was Monday afternoon and I'd just received a call from one of my supervisors that a seven-year-old Hispanic girl, Juanita, needed to be removed from a foster home and placed in another home. Juanita was slim, with short-cropped dark hair, an awkward but touching smile, and a lively demeanor. As the duty worker, I picked her up and loaded her things in my truck. I asked her if she wanted to say goodbye to her foster mother of several months. Almost as an afterthought, she casually waved one hand and said "bye" before walking out the door. As we drove away, I wondered if the girl knew she was leaving that home for good, rather than merely escaping for a day trip. Cognitively, she seemed to understand the permanency of her departure—at least it seemed that way from our conversation—yet she exhibited a very casual demeanor with her foster mother. I talked to her about the new home she was

moving to and asked about her thoughts for the future. Our exchange started off pleasantly, but when I tried to probe deeper, she didn't seem particularly willing to engage. Nothing went beyond superficial small talk.

When we arrived at the new foster home, her new foster mom and I helped her get settled in; we showed her around the house, placed her things in her new bedroom, and said our first greetings to the family members living there. As I took care of paperwork with her foster mom, Juanita seemed to be adjusting well. But at the end of that initial visit, as I prepared to leave, she threw her arms around me suddenly and said, "Don't leave me, you're the best friend I've ever had."

Of course, I was taken aback. Here I had known her for a twenty-minute car ride and the half hour it took to get her settled in to her new home, yet she had latched onto me as if I had known her for a lifetime. In the ensuing visits, the foster mother reported that the young girl latched onto everyone she came in contact with—the postal carrier, her classroom teachers, relatives of the family—in the same proprietary way.

Disinhibited RAD is quite common among children in U.S. child welfare systems and, as Juanita's story shows, one of its chief characteristics is a tendency to bond with strangers. Cases range in severity. Sometimes I see children with attachment concerns that do not meet the diagnostic category of RAD but still seem mildly troubled by their social relationships. Other times RAD can be so severe that I stand in wonder that the parents and children are still together at all.

Fortunately, there is hope for children with RAD. The more we learn about attachment theory, the more the evidence we find that attachment is a learned, transferable skill set. In my view, this is a more useful way of thinking about attachment than bonding theory, a popular model which holds that attachment disorders are the result of biological forces at birth. In the clinical environment bonding theory can be restrictive, for it tends to view a child's deficits as part of an irreparable condition, thereby depriving adoptive parents and children of the power to enact change. (An example of this deficit-oriented philosophy can be found in Verrier's 1993 work *The Primal Wound* discussed earlier.) Attachment theory, by comparison, is a strength-oriented model that understands relationships as socially learned habits and behaviors developed through appropriate interaction. This distinction is important because if attachments are learned, then children (and parents) who do not yet know how to attach can be taught to do so, given the right instruction. Moreover, if attachment is a transferable skill set, then any advances we make in a child's ability to attach likely will ease his transition into a new home. Likewise, when a foster parent helps a child connect to a new family that engages in healthy attachment patterns, that child will benefit.

Often when I am presenting at conferences about attachment issues in adoptive and foster families, clinicians approach me and ask if it is wrong for a child to be taught attachment skills with his foster parents, knowing that the child will eventually be placed in a new home. The simple answer is "no." Understanding that attachment is a transferable skill set rejects the deficit view of adoption in favor of a more hopeful framework that encourages adoptive and foster families to deal realistically with the problems at hand as they work to improve the parent-child relationship. The story of my son Danny speaks to that point:

> Until he was seventh months old, our sixth child, Danny, lived in a foster home with an older couple who specialized in caring for infants. As I mentioned earlier, they were incredibly wonderful foster parents, from whom I learned much about infant development. We made transitional visits for a couple of weeks until he had securely attached to us and was ready to go home. The transition went smoothly. A few months later, I was attending a Theraplay Conference in Chicago. After a full day of presentations, my family and I attended a backyard barbeque with several of the leaders of the Theraplay Institute. Chuck West, a widely-respected therapist who has worked with the Theraplay Institute since the

1970s, asked if he could hold Danny. With our permission, Danny curled into Chuck's arms and chest, immediately comfortable, and Chuck said, "This one knows how to nuzzle."

Children attuned to attachment know even from infancy how to respond to the physical and verbal cues of their caregivers. When it is cuddle time, they know how to cuddle. When it is time to respond to direction, they follow instructions to the tee. Danny's experiences with his foster parents had prepared him for his transition into our home. He had learned to "nuzzle" with his foster parents, a skill he could readily transfer to us as his adoptive parents. Danny has been able to develop a secure attachment with us because the rudiments of those skills began with the healthy foster parenting he received.

Attachment issues often arise in adoptive families because of the child's history of abuse and neglect, particularly in international adoptions and public child welfare adoptions. As you learn your child's attachment history, you can begin to attach to the child in a way that works within your family system. Likewise, as adoptive parents and therapists focus their attention on attachment issues within contemporary adoptive family systems, systemic family functioning is likely to show healthy improvement.

Summary

The attachment problems that may result from the adopted child's age of placement and placement history are important to consider when deciding to adopt. In general, research shows that younger ages of placement result in fewer emotional and behavioral problems, and, in turn, greater parental satisfaction. But children adopted at older ages can also lead to positive experiences and outcomes. It may take additional work and require therapeutic assistance, but most older children will respond positively to new parents, over time. Many years of clinical experience working with older, special-needs foster and adoptive children has taught me that these children need committed parents who can work with and endure the great challenges these children sometimes bring. Parents must be willing to seek therapy to help ensure a successful adoption experience.

If you are considering adopting older children, be aware that there is help available to ensure the success of the adoption experience. Although with most older, adopted children, there are attendant attachment struggles, newer therapy treatments such as Theraplay and Dyadic Developmental Psychotherapy (discussed as a treatment option later in this book) have demonstrated effectiveness in improving parent-child relationships. Before adopting, make sure to consider what range of ages, placement histories, and attachment concerns are acceptable to you as a family.

Chapter Six
Medical Special-Needs Children

One morning my wife, Allison, had some friends over at the house and was beginning a church meeting when the phone rang. On the other end was Julie, the placement worker from our adoption agency, who proceeded to tell me about an infant named Elijo Mendoza in need of a home. Elijo had been diagnosed with hypoplastic left heart syndrome (HLHS)—a congenital heart condition in which the left ventricle of the heart fails to develop properly. The disease is fatal if left untreated, but with a series of surgeries children can survive and, in many cases, lead normal lives. Elijo's birth mother was an undocumented farm worker who could not care for the child's medical needs, and Elijo was spending his nights in Stanford Hospital, in California's Bay Area, where he'd been for months. He'd already had the first of three heart operations. When Julie asked if we'd be interested in adopting him, I told her I'd get back to her later that day.

For the next few hours, Allison and I searched the Internet to find out everything we could about Elijo's heart condition. We were worried about Elijo's lifespan, his ability to play and engage in social activities, and the impact the disease would have on our other children. As busy parents, it was overwhelming to think of all the doctors visits which lay ahead, to consider the surgeries and in-home care we'd need to provide. Yet Allison and I had a pervasive feeling of love for this child and decided to go for it. Over the next several days we prepared a dossier of letters and other pertinent family information, what is known as a *home study,* and had Julie submit it into the pool of applications.

There were about fifty families seeking to adopt Elijo. The agency sought three criteria: (1) a stay-at-home mom who would have time to take the baby to his many medical appointments, (2) a family close to Stanford Hospital (or a comparable Bay Area children's hospital) so that his treatments could continue, and (3) a family with few or no children, so that the baby's immune system wouldn't be compromised by exposure to illness. Allison and I thought our chance of adopting Elijo was marginal, at best. Despite having previously adopted older children with emotional special needs (and my being a marriage and family therapist specializing in adoption) we met only one of the three stated criteria: Allison was a stay at home mom. My wife and I live in Coarsegold, a former mining town south of Yosemite National Park, and the closest children's hospital is about thirty minutes away. At the time we had five children ranging from six to twelve years old. From the agency's perspective, we had two very big strikes against us.

Every week or so we'd hear from our placement worker that the agency had cut the prospective parent pool down, and we were still in the running to adopt Elijo. As the weeks passed and the pool began to dwindle, we thought about how adopting a child with medical concerns would transform our lives. In addition to the frequent doctors visits, there would be the need to track Elijo's medication, to find babysitters attuned to his needs. Elijo's ability to engage in sports was another question. Would Elijo need physical therapy? Was it silly even to think he could participate in sports, given his heart condition? Though we were concerned about these and other issues, we decided that we were ready. In the end, the agency narrowed its selection to two families. As it happened, the second family, who lived in the Bay Area near Elijo's hospital, adopted the little boy—and we were not selected.

The outcome was disappointing, but the experience of being so close to adopting Elijo sparked my interest in adoptive children with medical special needs. It also prepared us for the adoption of our sixth child, Danny, just a few months later. Danny was born prematurely and in the beginning he had some medical concerns. Now, as an early toddler, he has successfully overcome them. The truth is that Danny's medical concerns are far less threatening than Elijo's and the experience of attempting to adopt Elijo more than prepared us for the health issues we have encountered. It gave us pause to consider and examine our family—recognizing what we could and could not handle—and opened our mind to the idea of adopting children who need extra assistance and care.

Unfortunately, our story belies the fact that children with medical problems are among the hardest to place. The range of diagnoses is diverse but the most common stem from prenatal drug exposure, congenital disorders, and injuries resulting from abuse. Because most statistical reporting in the United States is done on a state-by-state basis, the exact number of these children adopted each year is unknown. We do know, however, that the number of U.S. children with significant, chronic medical conditions is about 15 percent of the population, and that the number is growing.[1] It is estimated that 15 percent of the 500,000 foster children, or 75,000 children in U.S. child welfare systems, have medical conditions.[2] Although some of these children may be in the reunification process, many are in concurrent planning or already awaiting an adoptive home. When considering your adoption options, be clear about what you can and cannot accommodate in an adoption but recognize that a need exists. If your family can accommodate the medical special needs of children, you ought to consider this as a viable option.

Birth Parents' Medical History

In any adoption, you want to try and gather as much information as possible to make a good decision about whether or not to accept placement. This is especially true when adopting children with pre-existing medical conditions. Obviously, the severity of a child's medical concerns will vary, and some medical concerns will be more demanding than others. For that reason, you will want to obtain information about the birth parents' medical and neonatal history, as found in Figure 6.1.[3]

Medical conditions the birth parents may have at present, history of medical conditions, and diseases or mental illnesses in the birth parents' family histories, which may affect the child's physical, intellectual, social, and behavioral development.

Physical and demographic characteristics of the birth parents (e.g., height, weight, age, ethnicity, occupation, and education level).

Prenatal history documenting birth parents' use of alcohol, tobacco, other drugs, including over-the-counter and prescription medications. You will also want to know the level of prenatal medical care the birth mother received, obtain test results from substance use screening procedures administered during pregnancy, and determine the presence of any sexually transmitted diseases the birth mother may carry that could be transmitted to the child.

Cognitive impairments, if any, that the birth parents may have.

FIGURE 6.1 Essential information regarding birth parent's history

Child's Medical History

Regarding the child's medical history, you will want to obtain the information described in Figure 6.2.[4]•

Birth data such as weight, length, head circumference, Apgar (Appearance, Pulse, Grimace, Activity, Respiration) test results, and gestational length (full-term vs. premature).

Medical record and record of vaccinations/immunizations

Medical, psychological, dental, and emotional diagnoses, including the results of any medical, laboratory, or psychological tests already administered. This information should be in the medical record, but sometimes the record may be incomplete. You should ask verbally as a safety check.

Information about the child's development (e.g., gross and fine motor physical development, cognitive development, language development if older, and socio-emotional development). This should include milestones:

- Crawling
- Walking
- Running
- Feeding self with spoon
- First words
- Reactions to voices/presence of foster parents or other caregivers
- Knowledge of colors, letters, animal sounds
- Other age appropriate cognitive expectations

Physical or sensory impairments
Previous medical procedures, dental work, surgeries, therapies and other treatments that the child has already undergone
Histories of physical, sexual, or emotional abuse and/or neglect (because sometimes the abuse/neglect can cause long term medical complications)

FIGURE 6.2 Essential information regarding child's medical history

Once you have collected these materials, you also may wish to consult your doctor, dentist, social worker, and therapist, as well as any other accredited professionals who can help you make health predictions based on your child's diagnoses and history. Whether medical or psychological, many test results may be difficult to interpret correctly. Seeking assistance from professionals is critical. I also advise doing a bit of preliminary research on your own. The website KidsHealth.org, available at http://www.kidshealth.org/parent/pregnancy_newborn/medical_problems/medical_adopt.html is an excellent source of research-based information about children's medical problems. Developed by The Nemours Foundation, the website allows for article searches across a host of categories, from brain and nervous system disorders to allergies and the immune system.

---

* Figures 6.1 and 6.2 were adapted from the article "Medical Issues in Adoption," published by the Nemours Foundation/Kids Health. Copyright ©1995-2010. The full article is available at http://kidshealth.org/parent/positive/family/medical_adopt.html. Reprinted with permission.

Almost every state requires a Family Team Decision-Making meeting (or Team Decision-Making meeting) in which parents, service providers, community members and the child (unless it is deemed inappropriate) discuss the child's medical, social, and behavioral needs and appropriate placement options.[5] As proceedings move forward, prospective adoptive parents are brought into the FTDM. There, they are asked to consider the placement of the child for at least twenty-four hours before returning to proceed with the adoption, if still so inclined. If you are invited to a FTDM to discuss the placement of a child into your home, it is very important that you take that time to listen carefully to professional opinion about the child's needs. Try to be as honest as possible in assessing your family's capacity to meet those needs.

Family Team Decision-Making meetings can be very emotionally charged. When you see pictures of the child for the first time or when a child's adoption story is disclosed to you, it is easy to become carried away with noble sentiments, which dismiss the severity of the child's needs and concerns. Often parents feel gratitude to even be considered potential candidates. But do not eschew good judgment. Be certain to listen carefully, ask as many questions of the professionals as possible, and do not rush to decisions. Make sure to bring a copy of Figure 5.1 and Figure 5.2, as a reference. Something as important as adoption deserves the time it takes to make wise, responsible choices.

As discussed earlier, children in the adoption pool come with a variety of medical concerns. Domestic and international adoptions differ in these concerns. Domestically adopted children often sustain prenatal or post-partum exposure to alcohol, tobacco, and other harmful drugs. A number of these children may be victims of physical or sexual abuse and have scars, injuries, and emotional trauma requiring medical attention. Children with fetal alcohol syndrome (FAS), the clinical diagnosis for (1) brain damage, (2) impaired growth, and (3) head and face abnormalities resulting from a mother's alcohol use during pregnancy, are the most difficult to place. Infants who have been exposed to drugs or alcohol or who have been abused may show problems in intellectual, emotional, and behavioral development and it is important to seek clinical and therapeutic support for these issues. Below are other medical problems commonly found in domestic adoptions.

- Severe physical, mental, or emotional disturbances
- Ambulatory disabilities that prevent children from walking, even at older ages
- Heart conditions that require surgery for treatment
- Chronic diseases that require consistent monitoring and closely monitored medication dosages (e.g. diabetes)
- Impairments that necessitate the use of feeding tubes or other demanding treatments
- HIV or other blood-borne pathogens
- Deafness, blindness, or a combination
- Speech and language difficulties or delays
- Traumatic brain injury (TBI)
- Mental retardation or other pervasive developmental delays (e.g. autism)
- Orthopedic impairment

For children adopted internationally, complete medical histories are often much less available. Common medical problems often arise from poor institutional care in orphanages or the lack of available resources and medical services in the child's country of origin. Physical disfigurement is common. Cleft palates that are almost always surgically corrected in the U.S., might not receive proper treatment among children living abroad. Additionally, problems more typical in international adoptions such as malnutrition, lack of affectionate touch from caregivers, and the presence of untreated diseases, can stunt a child's physical, cognitive, and emotional growth and development.

Whatever their conditions, medical special-needs children need to be adopted by families with a high degree of sensitivity and compassion who are willing to make personal sacrifices for the sake of the child. Foster and adoptive parents seeking to adopt these children are often required to receive additional training beyond what is demanded of adoptive and foster parents at large. Social workers and public health nurses are important resources for parents. When adopting a child with a cleft palate, for instance, you can expect to receive help from a public health nurse specializing in feeding techniques. To take another example, if a child has Hepatitis C, the public health nurse might give you instructions at the FTDM, explaining the dangers of alcohol consumption to the child's vulnerable liver. In the case of emotional and behavioral problems related to physical abuse, trauma, or neglect, social workers and therapists can provide parents with valuable intervention strategies and supports.

Adoption assistance from the federal government for children with special needs is administered under the federal Title IV-E Adoption Assistance Program. Payments to parents of eligible children may take the form of either a one-time payment for adoption expenses up to $2,000, or ongoing payments until the child reaches maturity, usually understood as eighteen years old.[6] If a child qualifies for recurring AAP benefits, you can expect payments roughly equal to what the state or county was providing when the child resided in foster care.

According to a 2004 report of the Children's Information Gateway, children who qualify for Title IV-E adoption assistance also are eligible for monthly medical benefits under Title XIX (Medicaid).[7] In addition, states may offer additional services under Title XX, a flexible block grant that covers expenses for counseling, legal aid, respite care, and transportation services. For children who are not eligible for services under Title IV-E, state adoption assistance programs may cover some or all costs for medical treatment, associated therapy, rehabilitation, and special education.[8] In fact, states are required by law to provide health insurance to any child not eligible for Title IV-E assistance, whom the state has determined could not be placed for adoption without medical assistance.

Although states are responsible for notifying parents about the availability of adoption assistance under Title IV-E or state programs, the family must apply for such assistance through the state's local office. Adoption assistance programs are always administered by the county or state where the child was living when the adoption was formalized. However adoptive parents can continue to receive benefits for the child if they move to another state. In order to receive the full disbursement of benefits necessary to care for your child, it is important to have an advocate in your corner. Several years ago I was providing therapy for a child with severe behavioral and relational problems, which medical insurance often does not pay for. In this case, the parents requested I write a letter to the adoption assistance administrator in the boy's home state, explaining the diagnosis, the cost of treatment, and the estimated length of treatment. When I complied with their request, the parents were able to get an increase in their monthly benefits to cover the costs of much-needed therapy.

Summary
Couples who adopt children with special medical needs require support. They will have many visits to the doctor's office, prescription medicines, and daily care routines (e.g. feeding tubes, insulin shots) that demand time and energy. Though strenuous and occasionally frustrating, most parents of adopted children with medical special needs will tell you that their labor of love is rewarding. Support systems really are the key to success in these types of adoptions.

Consider the kind of support you have in your social relationships. As I mentioned, governmental assistance may be found in the form of social workers and public health nurses, as well as in adoption assistance funds set aside for children with medical special needs. However, adopting children with special medical needs often requires support beyond state and federal aid. Is your network of extended family and close friends the kind that can assist you? If you and your spouse need a break, could someone else help care for a child with special needs for an hour, a day, or a weekend? While some adoption and child welfare agencies do offer respite care services, it is important to have an extended network of family and friends who can provide some relief in a pinch.

You also need to be honest with yourself. Consider your ability to care for a child's medical problems. Could you change your life circumstances to accommodate a child who is blind or hearing impaired? If the child has cerebral palsy or a similar condition causing long-term physical or cognitive impairment, how would that change your life? The medical conditions of some children can be quite serious, including such diseases as HIV, hepatitis B, and hepatitis C. If you're considering adopting a child with one or more of these blood-borne pathogens, you'll need to research the illness thoroughly, to learn precautionary measures for the child's safety, your family's safety, and the safety of those in your social environment.

The sociologist H. David Kirk, a leading researcher in the adoption field, found that adoptive parents who acknowledge the difference between adoptive families and their biologically constructed counterparts tend to exhibit healthier functioning than those who reject such differences.[9] For parents adopting a child with medical concerns or other special needs, this recognition is particularly important. Adoptive parents of children with medical special needs must operate from a position of awareness. They must understand that these children will require special modifications for daily family living. Recognition of what lies ahead generally leads to healthier outcomes because parents take measures to plan and cope for the challenges they will inevitably face.

Chapter Seven
Parental and Prenatal Care History

I t is hard to imagine, but some parents are very abusive to their children. If you are like most prospective adoptive parents, you want a child so badly you could never imagine someone intent on doing harm to one. That makes it even more baffling when you get a call from your social worker, informing you that a child is available for adoption who has suffered abuse and neglect. Without understanding how a parent came to that decision, let alone how the child survived the abuse, your job as a new adoptive parent will be enormously challenging. To effectively parent a child who has endured abuse, you must first understand a few things about the psychology and behavior of the abused and the abuser.

Consider the case of Thomas, a nine-year-old African-American boy, for whom I provided therapy in my private practice. He was a foster child who had been placed in care because of his mother's drug use and the physical abuse he had endured when he was an infant. Since being placed in the system (which is how foster children refer to placement in child welfare systems), he had lived in seventeen different foster homes. In many of these homes, he endured physical—and in one case sexual—abuse by foster parents. He also exhibited severe behavioral problems (e.g., aggressiveness, anger, academic and social problems), which often led to his removal from the foster home. Thomas yelled in class, yelled at his foster parents, defied teachers, and instigated fistfights. He had nightmares and classic signs of attention-deficit/hyperactivity disorder (ADHD). When he came to me for therapy, he was currently in the care of a single, African-American foster parent who taught at his school. I will never forget his words to me when I introduced myself: "Thank you for taking my case. So many people say that their caseload is full, even when it's not. They just don't want to see me." This nine-year-old child seemed to understand, quite well, the inner workings of the child welfare system and its adjunctive services. State health insurance programs can be a royal headache for service providers and, as Thomas rightly understood, the unfortunate reality is most therapists simply do not want the extensive paperwork, low payment rates, and mind-numbing hassles associated with providing care to foster children under a deficient system.

I began to see Thomas in my office on a weekly basis. Because he suffered from reactive attachment disorder (RAD) and other mental health conditions, I started him on a regimen of Theraplay-based interventions. At first he seemed to be improving, but after a few weeks he relapsed into his typical behaviors: fighting and defiance at school, and belligerence at home. After an incident at school where Thomas fought with another student and then screamed at his teacher in front of the class, his foster mom lost control and physically abused him. Once again, from Thomas's perspective, the "system" had failed him. His social worker did her best: immediately intervening, reporting the abuse, and bringing Thomas in for an emergency session. For the foster parent, this meant relinquishing her job as a teacher and losing her legal right to care for foster children. For Thomas it meant placement in the home of a new set of foster parents—this time an elderly African-American couple who were very religious. As a couple, they'd been married many years and had raised their biological children to maturity with success. They felt pride in their parenting and eager to help Thomas, but also overwhelmed with the set of challenges he brought into the home. I could tell Thomas simply didn't trust them. So many people who ought to have kept him safe had failed him, including a state certified teacher, and he had a hard time believing his new foster parents' promises would be any different. He continued to test his parents with disruptive behaviors until they requested that he be removed from placement in their care.

For years, this cycle continued: each time Thomas entered a new home there was a brief honeymoon period in which everyone seemed to get along fine, but invariably he would test his parents, making it harder and harder for them to tolerate his behavior, until eventually they confirmed his worst suspicions—adults were not to be counted on. In the months that followed, Thomas's social worker and I became his greatest continuity as he "blew through" one foster placement after the next. Eventually, the agency ran out of potential foster homes appropriate for Thomas, and he was returned to the county social worker in the hope that other foster family agencies or group homes might better suit his needs. Although Thomas was making improvement in therapy, we couldn't keep a stable set of foster parents for him, even when we described his attachment problems to foster parents and told them the best treatment for Thomas—consistency and unconditional love—would gradually relieve his behaviors.

Granted, Thomas's behavioral problems were severe, but there was also a lack of understanding on the part of Thomas's foster parents about the kind of Intensive Treatment Foster Care (ITFC) he needed. Thomas displayed some of the classic attributes of a child who has suffered physical abuse for years. He wasn't just "born that way," his behavior problems were the direct result of the pathogenic care he received and what led to his diagnosis of reactive attachment disorder. Unfortunately, his life is unlikely to improve until he can find a permanent home and adoptive parents willing to ride out his behavior problems long enough to develop his trust.

Characteristics of an Abused Child

When I worked as a social worker for a foster family agency, I saw hundreds of children just like Thomas, children who were chronically abused or neglected, many showing evidence of multiple kinds of abuse. The disturbing truth is most abused children, in addition to being victimized by sadistic parents or parents unaware of proper discipline strategies to apply to these children, are the victims of multiple forms of mistreatment at the hands of their abusers: physical, sexual, verbal—unfortunately, nothing is out of bounds. In the remainder of the chapter, we will take a look at the most common forms of abuse and their associated symptoms. As a word of warning, the next few pages are unsettling at times. However they provide insight into the behaviors abused and substance-exposed children exhibit and are important to digest in the event your child has been a victim of abuse.

Physical Abuse

The Child Welfare Information Gateway, a reporting service of the U.S. Department of Health and Human Services, defines physical abuse as "any nonaccidental physical injury to the child."[1] Usually, but not always, physical abuse involves leaving a mark on a child in response to the physical violence. Examples of physical abuse include beating a child with an object (e.g., belt or switch); punching, slapping, kicking, shoving, or biting the child; pulling hair; and burning the child. Often instances of physical abuse are grotesque: in my caseload, I have seen severe injuries such as broken bones, burned genitals, scars from cigarette burns covering much of a child's body, and deep cuts inflicted on the child. This is to be distinguished from milder forms of physical discipline: "spanking and paddling, is not considered abuse, if it is reasonable and does not cause bodily injury."[2]

Children who have been physically abused tend to show outward signs such as unexplained bruises, marks, abdominal injuries, hair loss, bites, injuries, or lacerations. These injuries exist in varying stages of healing, from obvious new wounds to injuries that have disappeared with time. As a rule, children who have poor health, physical abnormalities, or developmental or personality disorders (oppositional defiance, hyperactivity, withdrawal) are more susceptible to being abused. Typically physically abused children are wary of parents or other adults. Teachers may notice a child making a habit of volunteering to stay after school to avoid going home. Often a child will exemplify extremes in behavior, shifting from hyperactive and aggressive one minute to overly compliant and clingy the next. In some cases the child may also exhibit a type of hypervigilance called "frozen watchfulness," where he will stare intently for prolonged periods, keenly observant of his surroundings. Some children may be suicidal. One of the most common symptoms of physical abuse is a tendency for the child to attribute their injuries to unlikely causes; in other words, the story just doesn't add up.

At older ages many of these children have chronic school problems and are routinely truant, running away, misusing drugs and alcohol, or both. This is especially true for teens in the child welfare system who have had negative experiences inside foster homes. Attending school just means running the risk of being placed back in a foster or group home, where they were subjected to maltreatment. Adoptive parents who accept physically abused children into their home need to be sensitive to the child's history. Not only should adoptive parents of physically abused children avoid any forms of corporal punishment, they should also be nonreactive to the challenging behaviors physically abused children use to test them. It is important to remain calm and consistently engaged even when your child is aggravating and rebellious.

Sexual Abuse

The Child Abuse Prevention and Treatment Act (CAPTA) defines sexual abuse as "the employment, use, persuasion, inducement, enticement, or coercion of any child to engage in, or assist any other person to engage in, any sexually explicit conduct or simulation of such conduct for the purpose of producing a visual depiction of such conduct; or the rape, and in cases of caretaker or inter-familial relationships, statutory rape, molestation, prostitution, or other forms of sexual exploitation of children, or incest with children."[3] A medical exam may reveal genital trauma, venereal disease, or pregnancy induced by forced sex.

Children who have been sexually abused typically have an overly sophisticated knowledge of sex for their age. As the child matures she frequently goes down one of two paths, in some cases becoming abstinent and strictly averse to sexual activity and other times engaging in sexual promiscuity and prostitution. Children, especially in younger ages, may develop sleep disturbances, night terrors, enuresis (bed-wetting), abdominal pain, appetite and weight disturbances, and a number of other problems resulting from the fear of sexual violence. We tend to see regressive behaviors, children acting young for their age, or withdrawing into a fantasy world. In the most severe cases, a sexually abused child may become suicidal or complain of psychosomatic illnesses related to bodily functions within the reproductive system. The lesson here is that the symptoms are diverse, and any time a child states that they've been sexually assaulted one must take those statements seriously.

In therapy I've worked with a number of victimized children. One ten-year-old girl, Amanda, was brought in by her parents. Adopted at birth, her upbringing had gone relatively well. However when her parents went on a trip, searching for a home in a new city, they left Amanda in the care of her uncle who sexually molested her. When they returned a week later they noticed that Amanda's behavior had changed dramatically. She had become moody—withdrawn, easily angered, and quick to cry. After three weeks she confessed to her mother what her uncle had done. The family immediately called the police and proceedings began against the uncle.

Amanda was brought in for counseling. For almost a year I worked with her and her mother. On a few occasions I met with the whole family, including Amanda's father and her siblings. The content of our sessions included several important points: (1) Amanda was not to blame for the uncle's actions; (2) Amanda had parents and siblings who could help her feel safe and secure; (3) it was normal for Amanda to feel a wide range of emotions such as anger and fear and; (4) Amanda was a person of great worth and potential.

In order for Amanda to avoid feelings of extreme repulsion toward sex or, conversely, the desire for sexual promiscuity, we also had to deal with Amanda's understanding of her own sexuality. On the basis of her family's values her mother and I explained to Amanda that sexuality is something that can be beautiful when one is older and in a loving, married relationship, however her uncle's sexual assault was a gross distortion of that sacred and healthy love.

Therapeutically, one of the keys to working with children who have been sexually abused is to restore their trust in adults. In Amanda's case, we used Theraplay to help her reconnect to her mother and other family members, so she could once again feel secure in their presence. Talking components of other models allowed us to examine Amanda's cognitive distortions and the intense feelings of self-incrimination ("It's my fault" or "I'm dirty"), fueling the erratic behavior she was displaying in front of her parents. After a volatile three-month period, she was beginning to feel healthy and more confident. However, changes like this rarely happen without the aid of professional counseling. If you adopt a child who shows signs of sexual abuse or confesses that abuse to you directly, the best thing to do is to seek professional support. Parents who work in concert with a therapist to facilitate healing from sexual abuse will likely need to focus on helping the child trust adults by being consistent and caring in their interactions with the child, by openly discussing concerns about sexuality in a sensitive yet forthright manner, and by assisting the child to enhance their sense of worth and self-confidence.

Verbal and Emotional Abuse

Verbal abuse always takes an emotional toll on the child but other unspoken kinds of emotional abuse, such as withholding affection or terrifying a child with a threatening demeanor, are equally damaging. On her website, Patricia Evans, author of *The Verbally Abusive Relationship,* gives a useful description of verbal abuse as "withholding, bullying, defaming, defining, trivializing, harassing, interrogating, accusing, blaming, blocking, countering, diverting, lying, berating, taunting, putting down, edifying, discounting, threatening, name-calling, yelling and raging."[4] According to the National Committee to Prevent Child Abuse, emotional abuse is a form of maltreatment that results in impaired psychological growth and development. This may include repeated attempts to ignore, isolate, belittle, or exploit the child, often because the parents or caregivers were emotionally abused themselves."[5]

Children who have been emotionally or verbally abused may develop abnormalities in their motor, speech, social, or intellectual development. It is also common for these children to display habit disorders such as thumb sucking, nail biting, rhythmic rocking of their body, or enuresis. As a parent, you may notice extremes in their behavior, from extreme passivity to extreme aggressiveness, from maturity to regressive, infantile behavior. Children who have been verbally or emotionally abused will often make derogatory comments about themselves or their behavior. In severe cases, they may make suicide attempts or discuss wanting to die.

When I ran a private practice in Illinois, a recently divorced mother brought in her eleven-year-old daughter, Mary, for therapy. A court order required the child to make visits to the father every other weekend. The mother described how the daughter would return from the visits to the father as "an emotional wreck." Frequently on weekend visits, Mary was not allowed to play with any friends or to leave the house. If she didn't behave as the father requested, he threatened to hurt or kill the family dog. He also warned that, if she didn't conform to his rules, he'd hurt her elderly grandparents who lived inside the home. To ensure that his daughter understood the threats, he would leave guns and rifles on her bed. Though he never hurt her or threatened her directly, he would punch holes in walls in front of her and threaten the people and animals she loved. By promising violence, he made a deliberate attempt to make the child feel unsafe.

The mother and daughter also told me of an incident in which the father had belittled Mary after a parent-teacher conference. In the course of the marking period, she had brought her grades up from Ds and Fs to Cs. The teacher and mom praised her improvement, but in the hallway afterwards the father yelled and screamed at his daughter, fuming that Cs were just not good enough and reminding her how stupid she was. Privy to the threats he had made, I immediately called Child Protective Services and filed a report of emotional abuse. Even with this information, they were hesitant to take the report because emotional abuse is so often difficult to prove. Still, I insisted. Eventually, the case went to court, the claim of emotional abuse was substantiated, and visits were discontinued.*

---

* However, in an unfortunate turn of events, the father appealed and won due to a strange aspect of Illinois law that does not recognize private practitioners as reliable witnesses in these matters. The last I heard, the mother was seeking custody and changes in visitation through family court since the children's court system had failed her.

Neglect and Abandonment

The Child Welfare Information Gateway defines neglect as the "failure of a parent, guardian, or other caregiver to provide for a child's basic needs."[6] These may include physical needs such as food, shelter, or supervision; educational needs such as special education classes; or the emotional needs required for the child's healthy psychological development.[7] Under CAPTA, "the failure to respond to the infant's life-threatening conditions by providing treatment (including appropriate nutrition, hydration, and medication) that in the treating physician's or physicians' reasonable medical judgment will be most likely to be effective in ameliorating or correcting such conditions" is considered a specific form of medical neglect.[8]

Children who have been neglected often are constantly hungry and exhibit signs of malnutrition: their skin may lack pallor and they may look gaunt and underweight. Without a proper diet, they may steal or beg for food. Unattended physical problems or injuries, poor hygiene, and abuse of alcohol or drugs are also quite common. Such children may have problems in school from missing classes or falling asleep during instruction. They may engage in delinquent behaviors or have thoughts of suicide. In many instances, the child simply states there is no one there to care for them.

Within the Child Protective Services (CPS) system, neglect and abandonment is often related to the birth parents' use of drugs and alcohol. In fact, in 2005, the National Center on Addiction and Substance Use at Columbia University estimated that "substance use is a factor in at least 70 percent of all reported cases of child mistreatment."[9] While the strength of the correlation is striking, it is not surprising that when parents are under the influence appropriate supervision and caretaking fall by the wayside. Often this is an extension of the lack of care the birth parents provided during the prenatal period when a mother's diet, health, and prenatal care are important to the child's outcome. Of course a pregnant mother's abstention from drugs and alcohol is doubly important because of the devastating effects substance use may have on the developing fetus.

Prenatal Drug and Alcohol Exposure

The word *teratogen* is an umbrella term used to describe any number of factors that have an adverse effect on the development of the fetus. Many things can be considered teratogens, including drugs, tobacco, alcohol, disease, medications, radiation, and other environmental pollutants. Among adopted children the most common teratogen exposure occurs because of the birth mother's use of drugs, tobacco, and alcohol during her pregnancy.

Legally, most states do not define the birth mother's consumption of drugs or alcohol during pregnancy as a form of child abuse. The idea that exposing a fetus to teratogenic substances is wrong stems mostly from a moral and public health standpoint rather than a legal perspective. It should be noted, however, that in 1997, in Whitner v. South Carolina,[10] the state supreme court sentenced Cornelia Whitner to eight years in prison for exposing her child to crack cocaine while she was pregnant. The ruling held that a pregnant mother who risks harm to a viable fetus may be prosecuted under state child abuse laws.[11]

---

* According to a report of the National Advocates of Pregnant Woman, every leading medical group to take a position on this issue, including the American Medical Association and the American Nurses Association, opposes the prosecution of pregnant mothers who use illegal drugs. Still, many women in South Carolina have been arrested without being offered drug treatment. Almost all have been African American. In the case of South Carolina v. Regina McKnight, the court charged Ms. McKnight with homicide, sentencing her to twelve years in prison after an autopsy revealed evidence of cocaine in the child's system.

Ira Chasnoff, the president of the Children's Research Triangle and a professor of clinical pediatrics at the University of Illinois College of Medicine in Chicago, is one of the nation's leading figures in the field of maternal alcohol and drug use during pregnancy as it relates to child development. In 2001, he authored an excellent book titled *The Nature of Nurture: Biology, Environment, and the Drug-Exposed Child,* in which he describes the impact maternal drug and alcohol abuse has had on the CPS system:

> Drug and alcohol abuse is among the most commonly named factors cited as contributing to the increase in child maltreatment, and almost all states report substance abuse is the dominant characteristic in child protective service caseloads. By 1990, the influx of drug-exposed infants into a system that already had a short supply of foster homes had stretched the substitute care system to its breaking point. Families that seek adoption through private agencies cannot avoid these problems. It is estimated that among babies available for private adoption domestically, slightly over half their mothers used alcohol or illegal drugs during pregnancy.[12]

Because the majority of children adopted through public agencies in the United States have had some type of prenatal exposure to alcohol or drugs (at least 70 percent according to The National Center on Addiction and Substance Abuse),[13] it is vital for adoptive parents to understand the long-term implications exposure may have on such children. While many complicated models can be used to determine the effect of teratogens on a developing fetus, in general there are four main variables which account for long-term child outcomes:

1. Type of substance
2. Dose amount
3. Time of exposure in the prenatal development period
4. Resilience (individual variation/genetic susceptibility)

Type of Substance

All drugs can have a damaging effect on the fetus when used during pregnancy; however, the ones that appear to be most devastating are the legal substances. Several kinds of prescription and non-prescription medications, including antibiotics, antidepressants, certain hormones, acne medicine (Acutane), diet pills, and high doses of aspirin are known to have adverse effects.[14] Alcohol consumption, even in minuscule amounts, can pose health and developmental risks to the fetus.[15] And although a mother's use of cocaine, methamphetamine, marijuana, and heroin is very dangerous in utero, it is the damage caused by legal drugs that is less understood by pregnant women and, thus, potentially more threatening. Fetal alcohol spectrum disorders (FASD) are the cluster of abnormalities found in the children of women who drink heavily during pregnancy. John Santrock, the author of a classic textbook on human development, describes the risks they pose to child's physical and intellectual development as the following:

> The abnormalities include facial deformities and defective limbs, face, and heart. Most children with FASD have learning problems and many are below average in intelligence with some that [have an intellectual disability]. . . . Even moderate drinking can have a negative effect on the offspring.[16]

Research suggests that caffeine may also be a problem. According to a recent study published in the *American Journal of Obstetrics and Gynecology,* pregnant women who consume 200 milligrams or more a day of caffeine—equivalent to two cups of instant coffee or a half to two cups of fresh coffee—show an increased risk of miscarriage.[17] And several studies have associated nicotine with an increased risk for preterm births, low birth weight, fetal and neonatal deaths, respiratory problems, and sudden infant death syndrome.[18] In short, it is evident that legal teratogens such as caffeine, alcohol, and nicotine have compromising effects on the developing fetus—and often on the adoptive child.

In the mid-1980s, researchers in the field of teratology expressed grave concern about the effect of cocaine on fetal development. Cocaine clearly has negative effects on children. Babies may be born with reduced birth weights and smaller head circumference; they may have impaired motor, language, and cognitive processing skills, and may show symptoms of withdrawal, including a high-pitched cry in infancy. However many of the dire predictions made about the outcomes of so-called "crack babies" never panned out. While no pregnant woman should ever use cocaine, children born to cocaine-addicted birth mothers seem to have better outcomes than children born with FASD. In your adoptive search, do not automatically assume that a child exposed to cocaine is destined for a lifetime of difficulty; for therapy can help manage many of the sensory processing disorders these children exhibit.[19]

Historically exaggerated predictions about cocaine-exposed babies have led those in the medical community to be more cautious in predicting the health risks associated with the newest generational fad of drug use: methamphetamines, or "meth," as it is widely known. One of the most comprehensive studies about long-term outcomes for meth-exposed babies comes from a group of New Zealand researchers led by Trecia Wouldes, a developmental psychologist and senior lecturer in the Department of Psychological Medicine at the University of Auckland.[20] Wouldes insists that when it comes to maternal methamphetamine use and its effect on child outcome, the medical community should not "rush to judgment" as in the past. At the same time, the study revealed that meth-exposed children had a greater propensity of physical deformities, including a smaller physical size, weight, and head circumference, and were at greater risk for cranial abnormalities and cleft palates. In terms of school performance, meth-exposed children appear to lag in math and language.

Before you consider adopting a child prenatally exposed to drugs or alcohol, carefully review the research, but understand that pregnant women who use legal drugs are often putting their children at greater risk than those who use illicit drugs. Further, most pregnant women who use teratogenic substances are using multiple substances, so it is hard to say what specific, isolated effects result from any single drug. Obviously one hopes that children are teratogen-free throughout fetal development, but the reality is most adopted children will have had some type of exposure. The good news is there are other protective factors. Even if the child you hope to adopt was prenatally exposed to teratogens, a low dose amount, a short time of exposure, and other resilience factors may give him a high chance for a healthy life.

Dose Amount
In the language of teratogens less is better: lower dose amounts of a drug or toxin, in general, have less effect on a developing fetus. Although there is no convincing evidence of a safe threshold of prenatal alcohol consumption, research indicates that serious effects such as low birth weight and mild disability can be seen at an exposure of roughly two alcoholic drinks per day; and most children who are believed to have the full expression of fetal alcohol syndrome are born to women drinking eight to ten drinks per drinking occasion, on a regular, often daily basis.[21] Be sure to find out the amount of the drug or toxin the child has been exposed to. This is useful information in your decision-making and should be interpreted with the help of an informed pediatrician.

Time of Exposure in the Gestational/Developmental Period
Another critical piece of information to verify is when in the child's gestational development he was exposed to the teratogen. If

this information is available, you will likely receive it in the Family Team Decision Making (FTDM) meeting or when your social worker presents a child to you along with the child's case file. The first couple weeks of fetal development (germinal period) tend to see low levels of susceptibility to teratogens, but weeks three through nine (embryonic period) are the time of greatest sensitivity.[22] For the remainder of the pregnancy (fetal period), the child shows moderate levels of sensitivity to teratogens.

Research shows it is possible to pinpoint what organs or appendages will be affected based on when those physical features are developing.[23] For example, the fetal ears primarily develop during weeks 4 to 16 and the ear's greatest susceptibility to harmful teratogens occurs during weeks 4 to 9, with moderate susceptibility from weeks 10 to 16. So if the birth mother is drinking alcohol in weeks 2 or 3, it probably won't affect the ears, although it may affect the heart and nervous system. If you are considering adopting a substance-exposed child, be sure to inquire as to the timing of the child's exposure, for this can make a tremendous difference. If this information is not available from the social worker or other professionals at the FTDM meeting, then consult with your pediatrician when you first have the child examined.

Resilience

Children each have their own level of resiliency, and this includes the capacity to withstand teratogenic exposure during fetal development. Some degree of resiliency may be related to genetics, although how much is uncertain: resiliency is a factor that is revealed over time as the child matures and we come to understand how protective factors such as parental attachment and comfort in school may magnify or counteract the impact of exposure.

Whether they are exposed to teratogens or the victims of abuse, children are astounding in their drive to heal from the traumas they've faced. According to one study, Child Protective Services agencies in the United States receive more than 50,000 reports of suspected child abuse or neglect each week. As a result of investigations into these reports, researchers estimate that approximately 896,000 children have been victims of abuse or neglect—an average of more than 2,450 children per day.[24] For many of these children, mental health problems resulting from the abuse are compounded by long-term emotional and behavioral disorders which arise from prenatal drug and alcohol exposure. In a longitudinal study, the clinical psychologist Ann Streissguth and her colleagues at the University of Washington School of Medicine found that by adulthood 90 percent of alcohol-exposed children had mental health problems, 60 percent had a disrupted school experience, 50 percent had been confined in the criminal justice system, 49 percent had displayed inappropriate sexual behavior, and 35 percent had substance use problems.[25] Yet over and over I see children who are the exception rather than the rule. I can only attribute this to the powerful spirit and tenacity of youth, the somewhat intangible quality of childhood resiliency.

Characteristics of Abuse and Abusers

The U.S. Department of Health and Human Services, Administration for Children and Families, publishes some of the most recently available statistics about child abuse in the United States. According to a report titled *Child Maltreatment 2005,* "62.8 percent of victims experienced neglect, 16.6 percent were physically abused, 9.3 percent were sexually abused, 7.1 percent were psychologically maltreated, and 2 percent were medically neglected. In addition, 14.3 percent of victims experienced such 'other' types of maltreatment as 'abandonment,' 'threats of harm to the child,' or 'congenital drug addiction.'"[26] When it comes to neglect, physical abuse, and psychological maltreatment, parents are the most likely to victimize a child, accounting for 76.5

percent of physical abuse, 86.6 percent of neglect, and 80 percent of psychological maltreatment. When it comes to sexual abuse, parents are less often the culprits. They are convicted in only 23.6 percent of all U.S. cases. The most frequent perpetrators of sexual abuse were "other relatives" (28.7%), followed by "other[s]" (23.3%), and finally "friends and neighbors" (4.9%).[27] In direct contrast to other forms of abuse, in cases of sexual abuse those who have little formal responsibility for the care of the child represent the greatest risk for carrying out the abuse.

Meeting an Abusive Parent

Unfortunately, as a prospective adoptive parent, there is a very realistic chance you will have to deal with abusive or heedless birth parents at some stage in the process. If you are doing concurrent planning as part of an adoption through the child welfare system, this may occur early on in the foster parenting phase. In a private agency adoption, you are more likely to meet with a birth parent after placement, on discovery that the child's mother, though not abusive under most applications of U.S. law, used alcohol or drugs during the pregnancy. In an international adoption, your visit to the child's country of origin may mean encountering birth parents who abandoned their child in an orphanage. Keep in mind that caregivers who mistreat or dispossess children often grew up in homes where they were themselves abused, deprived, abandoned, or witnesses to violence.[28] In many cases, victims of abuse fail to develop effective coping mechanisms for dealing with their children's behavior problems because of poor parental role models; homes in which violence and perpetration of abuse were acceptable mechanisms for gaining power and control. Furthermore, we often find that abusive parents have their own mental health issues or psychopathology: depression, substance misuse and dependency, or specific delusions about harming a child.[29]

When I was a social worker we had a poster in our break

room describing ten behaviors, which, though annoying, suggest a child is developmentally okay. One of the apothegms has always stood out to me: "Four-year-old children are notorious for spilling their milk at the dinner table." Cognitively, four-year-olds believe they are capable of reaching for the cup and successfully navigating it to their mouth, but their gross and fine motor development are not as advanced as their mind conceives. So inevitably they spill their milk. Abusive parents who have unrealistic expectations and lack knowledge about child development will berate or assault a four-year-old child for the accident, attributing the spill to the child's stubbornness or stupidity. Obviously this is not the best approach to parenting.

However when interacting with abusive parents one must understand that there are often underlying environmental or historical factors responsible for the abuse and that taking a confrontational attitude will do little to improve the situation. If a parent has a long-term, chronic illness, lives in poverty or economic deprivation, or experiences significant losses in their life such as a death in the family, he will be more likely to abuse a child. In your interactions it is best to be civil, finding comfort in the fact that as an adoptive parent you can choose a different approach in raising the child.

Summary

There are several methods of play therapy such as Theraplay that are effective for treating abused children. In some of these models, children are allowed to grow and heal at their own pace through the child's symbolic use of toys and play activities. In other models, children are directly engaged with their parents in building healthier attachments. In a later chapter, we'll take a look at therapy options in detail, including what to look for in a therapist providing post-adoption services. For the time being, trust that when you adopt a child who has been abused, you are not alone.

Most children seem to have an innate drive towards happiness. They want to play, they want to be loved, and they want to believe that life will be good. Abuse can temporarily disguise this natural good will, making children seem wary and fearful, or leaving in its wake the lingering distrust of attachment disorders. But encouraging, consistent parenting when coupled with professional therapy can restore hope in a child and eliminate many of the behavioral problems we tend to find. As a parent of several adopted children with difficult backgrounds, I feel a sense of purpose in this cause: giving children the opportunity to find health and hope.

Chapter Eight
Demographic Variables and Life Chances

The German sociologist Max Weber coined the term *life chances* used in the social sciences when describing how a person's opportunities for social, political, and economic upward mobility can be statistically predicted based on variables such as race, class, and gender. Whenever we talk about an adopted child's potential to acquire knowledge, form secure emotional attachments to peers and parents, and develop skills required to be a productive member of the workforce, we are in essence trying to qualitatively predict that child's life chances. That is why when it comes to adoption factors such as age of placement, medical and behavioral conditions, prenatal substance exposure, and the experience of abuse are such important considerations. While there's no way to foresee the future, the knowledge that as parents we can reasonably predict adoption outcomes based on a few critical variables provides a certain level of comfort when making decisions.

Realistically, only you know what you can and cannot handle, and only you know what are acceptable outcomes with regard to your expectations for adoption. You may find joy in adopting a child with severe mental and medical handicaps, welcoming the chance to make a difference in the life of a child with extreme needs. For another couple this same experience might seem overwhelming and completely outside their capacity. In the end, your happiness with the adoption experience really depends on your expectations and what you are willing to sacrifice for the child's best interest.

Specific variables such as race, gender, country of birth, and foster care placement history affect a child's life chances in important ways, including the child's likelihood of being adopted. Children of color, children from low-income families—and to some extent male children—are disproportionately more likely to languish on the child welfare rolls. This is especially true if these children are older, belong to a large sibling group, or have behavioral problems or other special needs such as medical concerns or developmental delays. These children are often referred to as "hard-to-place" simply because of the demographically sensitive supply and demand nature of the adoption market.

Prospective adoptive couples can take a number of proactive measures to prepare for adopting children of a different race or ethnicity. Doing so requires parents attain a sufficient degree of *cultural competency*—what sociologists describe as our ability to relate to and interact with people of cultures and backgrounds different than our own. As the trend toward transracial adoptions has grown, adoptive parents have had to be increasingly savvy about ethnic and cultural issues their child may face, particularly when among peers.

A study by Roy Bean, a professor of marriage and family therapy at Brigham Young University, and his colleagues suggests that there are three critical components to cultural competency: (1) our own *awareness* of the values and beliefs that stem from our own cultural background (2) the *knowledge* or *worldview* we have of cultures different from our own, and (3) appropriate sensitive *behaviors* or strategies for how to interact with others from differing backgrounds based on our awareness and knowledge.[1]

Similarly, the U.S. Department of Health and Human Services Office of Minority Health defines cultural competency as

> ... a set of congruent behaviors, attitudes, and policies that come together in a system, agency, or among professionals that enables effective work in cross-cultural situations. 'Culture' refers to integrated patterns of human behavior that include the language, thoughts, communications, actions, customs, beliefs, values, and institutions of racial, ethnic, religious, or social groups. 'Competence' implies having the capacity to function effectively as an individual and an organization within the context of the cultural beliefs, behaviors, and needs presented by consumers and their communities.[2]

Here "culture" refers to a broad set of demographic categories, including but not limited to race. Culture might constitute the culture of age, the culture of the foster care system, the culture of disabilities, or other additional variables beyond a child's ethnic or racial background. However, most of the research literature and government work has been directed at cultural competency with respect to race.[3]

Where this definition applies to you—if you are a prospective adoptive parent considering adopting a child of a different race or ethnicity—you need to first examine your own values and beliefs. What habits, modes of communication, forms of expression, and core philosophies inform and enrich your culture? How do these beliefs shape your understanding of the world and influence the way you will raise your child? Once you have investigated your own cultural identity, it becomes easier to build knowledge about less-familiar cultures whose customs you may not readily appreciate. Cultural competency does not mean relinquishing your own cultural practices, it simply means exhibiting sensitivity to the cultural history of the child. In my own experience, as a Caucasian married to a woman of Mexican-American descent, it has been a privilege to adopt children who are partially Mexican American and partially Caucasian, as well as one son who is of Guatemalan origin. Marrying my wife and adopting children with Hispanic backgrounds has enriched my cultural awareness in a number of ways—from helping me learn about the importance of extended family cohesiveness in the Mexican-American community to introducing me to an entirely new cuisine and a range of lifestyle and political beliefs different from my upbringing.

From the time of our first adoption, Allison and I have made a concerted effort to support our children's efforts to maintain a connection to their cultural heritage. However that has not always been easy. When we moved to Illinois we enrolled our children in a school district that was predominately white, where they literally doubled the ethnic diversity of the student population. That made it difficult for them to understand their ethnicity, and at various times they've each asked me to identify their race. I'll never forget the round-and-round attempt to explain to one of my sons, age six at the time, that he wasn't "black" as he claimed to be. In the Midwest, Hispanics, Asians, Polynesians and other minority children are often lumped into the general category of "black" by children unaware of subtler racial and ethnic distinctions. Helping my children navigate minority identity as a white father in a Midwest culture was complex, to say the least. It was part of the reason I wanted to return to California. I hoped that by being closer to extended family and other minorities in the community my children would be exposed to a wider ethnic diversity and better understand their Hispanic identity and heritage.

According to Betsy Vonk, a professor of social work at the University of Georgia, parents need to be conscious of their own level of racial awareness for transracial adoptions to be successful.[4] They need to take time to develop a multicultural plan designed to help the child grow up with a congruent sense of cultural identity and background. As children age, parents will continually need to reinforce the survival skills that allow these children to cope with the prejudice and bigotry they may face in school, in the work-force, and in relationships throughout their lives.

Adoption outcome studies generally support the practice of transracial adoption. Arnold Silverman, a professor of sociology at SUNY-Nassau Community College, has written prolifically over his career about the long-term development of transracially adopted children. Silverman found that 75 percent of transracially adopted preadolescent and younger children adjusted well in their new homes.[5] Similarly, researchers from the Search Institute in Minneapolis reported that transracial adoption was not adverse to adopted children in several key indicators of emotional and behavioral health, including self-esteem, academic achievement, peer relationships, and parental and adult relationships.[6]

In spite of this evidence, transracial adoption has a number of critics. Owen Gill and Barbara Jackson's book *Adoption and Race: Black, Asian, and Mixed Race Children in White Families,* published in 1983, was one of the first to outline the problems encountered when minority children are raised in White families.[7] Chiefly, the book's arguments are as follows: (1) transracial adoption is discriminatory to the Black community by taking their most precious resource—their children, and (2) Caucasians lack the ability to prepare minority children for the racial discrimination and challenges they will inevitably face.

Presently, there is little research to bear out these conclusions, yet significant portions of the leadership in the social work profession—the most prominent example being the National Association of Black Social Workers (NABSW)—maintain that children should be adopted by couples or individuals who are the same race as the child.[8] Part of their argument addresses institutional discrimination the organization justifiably contends is responsible for African-American children being detained by Child Protective Services at disproportionate rates. Moreover, NABSW points out that legal shifts to make adoption more readily available—such as the Multiethnic Placement Act of 1994, the Interethnic Placement Act of 1996, and the Adoption and Safe Families Act of 1997—actually mask racial discrimination and should be repealed. Transracial adoptions should only occur, NABSW claims, after documented evidence indicates that suitable minority parents of the same race as minority children cannot be found. Essentially, this is a policy of transracial adoption as a "last resort."

And although there is no question there are benefits to having a child raised by adoptive parents of the same race, the staggering number of children in desperate need of a home makes transracial adoption a necessity. NABSW notes that African-American families adopt children at a higher rate than other ethnic groups, and such efforts should be applauded—yet every race and ethnic group should be granted the right to adopt children of color. Norval Glenn, a sociologist at the University of Texas, has repeatedly argued for a "child-centric" society, wherein the first priority is satisfying the child's need for a nurturing set of caregivers.[9] The reality is that transracial adoptions satisfy the need for "hard-to-place" children to find placement in a safe and loving home.

Becoming a Culturally Competent Parent

At this point you may be asking yourself, "Do I have what it takes to adopt a child that is older, has special needs of some kind, or is a different ethnicity than myself?" Only you know the answer to that. Professional therapists and counselors can sometimes offer advice on this question, but evaluating your capacity to parent a child is ultimately an individual or family responsibility. There is much to learn but one of the keys to success, if you are willing to adopt a "hard-to-place" child, is to increase your level of cultural competency. Figures 8.1–8.3[10] provide a good diagnostic tool to evaluate your baseline level of cultural competency. The goal is not to attain a minimum number of "yes" responses in order to attain competency, but rather to use the charts as a basis for continual reflection and improvement.

*There are twelve recommendations concerning racial aware-
ness for transracial adoptive (TRA) parents. They are related
to self- and other awareness, as well as sensitivity to racism.*

1. I understand how my own cultural background influences
   the way I think, act, and speak.
2. I am able to recognize my own racial prejudice.
3. I am aware of stereotypes and preconceived notions that I may
   hold toward other racial and ethnic minority groups.
4. I have examined my feeling and attitudes about the birth
   culture and race of my children.
5. I make ongoing efforts to change my own prejudiced attitudes.
6. I have thoroughly examined my motivation for adopting a
   child of a different race or culture than myself.
7. I am knowledgeable of and continue to develop respect
   for the history and culture of my children's racial heritage.
8. I understand the unique needs of my child related to his or
   her racial or cultural status.
9. I know that transracial-cultural adoptive parenting involves
   extra responsibilities over and above those of in-racial parenting.
10. I have examined my feelings about interracial dating
    and marriage.
11. I know that others may view my family as "different."
12. I know that my children may be treated unkindly or unfairly
    because of racism.

FIGURE 8.1 Racial awareness

---

* Figures 8.1, 8.2, and 8.3 originally appeared in the article "Cultural Com-
petence for Transracial Adoptive Parents" by Elizabeth Vonk, published in
Social Work, Vol. 46, no.3 (July 2001):246-55. Used by permission of the
National Association of Social Workers.

Many suggestions have been made to TRA parents to build a bridge between their own and their child's race and culture. The following fourteen recommendations vary in terms of how direct a link they provide to the child's birth culture.

1. I include regular contact with people of other races and cultures in my life.
2. I place my children in multicultural schools.
3. I place my children with teachers who are racially aware and skilled with children of my child's race.
4. I understand how my choices about where to live affect my child.
5. I have developed friendships with families and individuals of color who are good role models for my children.
6. I purchase books, toys, and dolls that are like my child.
7. I include traditions from my child's birth culture in my family celebrations.
8. I provide my children with opportunities to establish relationships with adults from their birth culture.
9. I provide my children with the opportunity to learn the language of their birth culture.
10. I provide my children with the opportunity to appreciate the music of their birth culture.
11. I have visited the country or community of my child's birth.
12. I have demonstrated the ability for sustained contact with members of my child's racial or ethnic group.
13. I seek services and personal contacts in the community that will support my child's ethnicity.
14. I live in a community that provides my child with same-race adult and peer role models on an ongoing basis.

FIGURE 8.2 Multicultural planning

Perhaps because of the need to tailor a response to a specific situation, recommendations for survival skills seem to lack specificity in the professional literature. Literature aimed toward adoptive parents rather than professionals contains suggestions that are somewhat more concrete. The following thirteen items vary in specificity.

1. I educate my children about the realities of racism and discrimination.

2. I help my children cope with racism through open and honest discussion in our home about race and oppression.

3. I am aware of the attitudes of friends and family members toward my child's racial and cultural differences.

4. I am aware of a variety of strategies that can be used to help my child cope with acts of prejudice or racism.

5. I know how to handle unique situations, such as my child's attempts to alter his or her physical appearance to look more like family members or friends.

6. I help my children recognize racism.

7. I help my children develop pride in themselves.

8. I tolerate no biased remarks about any group of people.

9. I seek peer support to counter frustration resulting from overt and covert acts of racism toward my children, my family, or me.

10. I seek support and guidance from others who have a personal understanding of racism, particularly those from my child's race or birth culture.

11. I have acquired practical information about how to deal with insensitive questions from strangers.

12. I help my children understand that being discriminated against does not reflect personal shortcomings.

13. I am able to validate my children's feelings, including anger and hurt related to racism or discrimination.

FIGURE 8.3 Survival skills

Evaluating your own cultural competency is only a starting point. There are many organized ways of working to enhance competence, both for the parent and the child. As a member of the editorial board for *Adoption Quarterly*, a scholarly journal devoted to the issues of adoption, I recently reviewed an article about Caucasian parents who had adopted Korean children.[11] As reported in the article, the adoptive parents sent their adoptive children to Korean heritage camps, where the children learned about their country of origin while interacting with transnational adopted children in recreational activities promoting ethnic pride. Researchers explored the impact the Korean heritage camp had on the children's racial awareness and identity once they reached maturity. A qualitative review of interviews of the Korean adoptees revealed that from the children's perspective "although camps were fun, they did not impact their sense of identity significantly because they did not do *enough* to address the racial challenges they faced." While it helped them gain a rudimentary understanding of their culture, the now-grown children wished the camps had done more to help them confront the ostracizing remarks and experiences of racism they had encountered growing up. What is particularly interesting is that the main reason the parents sent the children to camp—to help their children feel less ethnically isolated through exposure to other Korean children adopted by Caucasian families—was the very issue the camp failed to adequately remedy.

The lesson is not that the heritage camp is without merit, rather that sending children away for a few weeks out of the year is insufficient as a means for transracial adoptive children to sort through questions of racial and ethnic identity. Developing cultural competency is an ongoing process that requires consistent efforts on the part of the parents to ensure appropriate racial and ethnic identity development. Kaye Nelson, a professor of counselor education at Texas A&M University, Corpus Christi, and her doctoral student, Cloe Lancaster, recently reported that the adoptive parents' commitment to cultural socialization can significantly impact the children's perceptions of racial identity and social adjustment.[12] For children to feel comfortable, transracial adoptive parents have to get personally involved in deepening their own cultural competence and in educating children about the children's ethnic heritage and the current or future discrimination they may face.

From practice and research, I know that many adoptive parents strive to educate their internationally adopted children in the country and culture of their origin, as well as deepen their own cultural competence. During the 1990s, Dave Wesson, an adoptive father I interviewed for my dissertation, along with his six grown siblings and their spouses adopted more than twenty Romanian children. The family recognized a need for willing parents to come to the aid of displaced children following the late-1989 collapse of the Ceausesco regime. At that time between 100,000 and 300,000 children were abandoned or sent to state-run orphanages, many of the children in poor physical health, diagnosed with infectious diseases, and facing severe growth and developmental impairments.[13]

After adopting the children and bringing them to the United States, the Wesson family immediately became active in the young children's lives. Dave Wesson's two sons were young and had no apparent physical or emotional difficulties, however several of the children adopted by the extended family had unique medical needs, including autism and developmental delays requiring clinical support. In addition to finding therapeutic services for their children, the extended Wesson family would plan social outings to fraternize, sing, and learn about Romania. The father even planned a trip back to Romania, so that the boys, in their teenage years, could better understand their country of origin. Most recently, the father has co-founded a non-profit foundation that gives humanitarian service to help others adopt internationally.

Admittedly, the Wesson family's commitment to their children's Romanian heritage is exceptional. However the story illustrates one crucial reality: improving cultural competence is not easy; it demands full immersion in the child's life, dedication to extend the network of friends, relatives, and organizations who share the child's national or ethnic heritage, and a commitment to seek new cultural experiences side by side with the child. As it turns out, the Wessons' experience would be difficult to replicate today. In 2004, after allegations of corruption by adoption officials, Romania passed a law banning adoptions of all children under the age two, and placing severe restrictions on older-age, international adoptions.[14] However, with the large number of minority children and other demographically "hard-to-place" children waiting for an adoptive home here in the United States, families need not lament the loss of adoption options in Romania and other countries abroad. Currently, we need more families willing to adopt abandoned, neglected, and developmentally impaired children inside a U.S. child welfare system rife with its own set of institutional hazards.

Statistics about Waiting Adoptable Children

In 2006 the U.S. Department of Health and Human Services Administration for Children and Families published the *Adoption and Foster Care Analysis and Reporting System* (AFCARS),[15] a detailed demographic analysis of the U.S. adoption and foster care system. Data from the AFCARS report reveal that in 2003 there were approximately 520,000 children in the foster care system. About 120,000 of those children were awaiting adoption. On average these children were removed from the birth parent's home at age five and had been waiting on child welfare rolls for almost four years; the average age of a waiting child was nearly nine years old. The AFCARS report indicates, further, that 40 percent of the adoptable children waiting for a suitable home are African American, followed by 37 percent Caucasian, and 14 percent Hispanic. These children reside mostly in non-relative foster care (55%), followed by pre-adoptive homes (17%) and relative foster care (16%).

At first glance, one can't help but recognize the need is tremendous, particularly for African-American children. The evidence is even more compelling when we account for the number of public adoptions that occur outside the child welfare system. In an average year, only 50,000 adoptions are completed through U.S. child welfare systems—that's only 10 percent of the population in care and less than 42 percent of children who have been deemed "adoptable." Worse still, African-American children constitute only 33 percent of all adoptions even though 40 percent of children waiting for adoption are Black. Our federal, state, and local governments are seeking to rectify the situation; parents of 87 percent of all publicly adopted children earn a subsidy. Yet that hasn't been enough incentive to meaningfully tilt the balance of the disproportionate numbers of minority, older, and special-needs children on the child welfare rolls. We simply need more open-minded parents willing to adopt children who are waiting for a home.

Summary

There's no question that developing cultural competence takes work. Day after day you will need to make a consistent, highly focused effort to reinforce the emotional and behavioral regulation skills the child will need to possess in order to overcome social obstacles. Children of color will almost certainly experience discrimination and bigotry at some point in their lives. They will have to field inquiries about private matters when others discover that their parents are of a different race. Other children whose experiences and backgrounds make them similarly difficult to place, including low-income children, older children, children with low IQs, and children with special medical and behavioral needs, may also present unique challenges.

Despite the additional work and effort that may be required to make such adoptions successful, there is plenty of encouraging research that demonstrates parents can raise these children into confident, high-achieving adults. With effort, you can increase the "life chance" for these children—giving them the foundational guidance they need for a promising future.

Chapter Nine
Human Development and Adoption

No book about adoption would be complete without exploring how life-cycle developmental issues, particularly those rooted in identity formation, impact adoption experiences. For adopted children, the construction of identity is crucial to mental health stability and achieving the best trajectory for social and emotional development. By examining these issues from a systemic perspective, we can begin to understand how adoption is beneficial to adoption triad members.

There is no doubt birth parents benefit from adoption in important ways. When a birth parent selects adoption they are more likely to complete their education, less likely to experience developmental setbacks due to parental neglect, and more likely to marry someone and obtain the known benefits marriage affords to men and women.[1] All of these factors become more meaningful when birth parents are teens, yet few teenagers give up their babies for adoption.* In 1969 approximately 25 percent of unwed births resulted in adoption. In 1991, that

---

* Clinically, birth mothers who select childrearing rather than adoption tend to be ignored by parents, who focus their efforts on helping the new baby. By neglecting their teen child these parents fail to finish the job of nurturing their daughter's emotional needs. As a result the teen mother's development is stunted, and she is much less likely to finish her education and later marry.

number was down to 4 percent.[2] Other researchers estimate the current range of unwed births resulting in adoptions to be somewhere from 2 to 5 percent.[3] Understanding why that is—and raising awareness among teenagers that adoption may be a wise decision in adolescence—requires a closer look at the complexity of relationships that occur inside a family.

Typically, when a teenage girl becomes pregnant, the greatest obstacle to adoptive placement is the adverse reaction of the young woman's parents, who do not want to lose their grandchild. If the teen mother chooses to raise the child, whether on her own or with assistance from her parents, emphasis is often placed on the baby to the neglect of the continuing developmental needs of the teenager. The teen mother is left to develop an identity around motherhood, not selfhood.

Later in life, many former teen mothers lack awareness about the nature of their identity and remain uncertain as to their personal interests, opinions, and talents. They know how to behave in other roles in their lives—as mothers, wives, employees, and daughters—but their sense of self and identity formation are stunted as a result of premature pregnancy and early transition into a maternal role that requires attention to the newborn's feeding and hygiene needs, as well as hours devoted to nurturing, affection, and coddling. The reality is that teen mothers often miss out on a range of issues that are part of normal teen development, such as working a part-time job, playing an instrument, or beginning to form their religious and political views. Upon entering adulthood, these young mothers often struggle with depression and have difficulty with couple and familial roles because they never completed the teenage developmental tasks of identity formation.

The choice of adoption may allow teens additional time to mature into the role of motherhood. When a young woman makes an adoption plan, the teenager's parents may focus on helping the young woman achieve the developmental milestones of completing high school, finding independent housing, and enrolling in college or entering the workforce. The teen and her parents both can be more available on an emotional level, listening to each other with greater empathy because they are not preoccupied with the demands of caring for a newborn.

Unfortunately, though, in many cases the extended family actually discourages adoptive placement. Teen mothers are often shamed or ostracized when the pregnancy is discovered, a process one famous marriage and family therapy pioneer, Murray Bowen, calls "emotional cutoff."[4] Immediately after the child is born, the extended family members want to coo and coddle the baby, welcoming the newborn into the family. Forgiveness is extended for the early pregnancy, or the pregnancy's timing is denied or overlooked, as the mother is emotionally reunited with her family. The baby helps win the affection of the extended family, and at the same time becomes the mother's ticket of re-admission back into the good graces of the family of origin. Few teen mothers will select adoption, knowing it may mean sacrificing the opportunity for acceptance from their family, so the extended family and family of origin members become deterrents to adoptive placement.

In order for adoption to seem like a legitimate option for a teenage mother, the process of emotional cutoff and re-admission needs to be addressed therapeutically in a family systems context. Bowenian Family Systems Theory is one effective method. Bowen's theory, one of the most comprehensive in the marriage and family therapy field, suggests that our emotional reactivity increases when we lack an awareness of self. Because we are immersed in the habits and rituals in which our families grew up, we aren't always conscious of dysfunctional patterns that lead to impulsive emotional reactions. As we become more self-aware of our intrapsychic and relational patterns, we tend to exhibit responses that are proactive, not reactive. Bowen calls this awareness "differentiation of self."[5] Appropriately applied during pregnancy to the extended family and teenage mother, Bowenian therapy frees the young woman to make pregnancy resolution strategies of her own accord. Parents and other family of origin members thus may focus on the continuing developmental needs of the pregnant teen, rather than the soon-to-be adopted child.

For expectant adoptive parents, the time between hearing news of an adoptive match and introducing a new child into the home is usually a period of weeks or months, and in some cases just days or hours. Whether an infant, toddler, or older child is being placed into an adoptive home, first-time adoptive parents will need to make huge adjustments in their transition to parenthood. All parents must make profound changes in preparation for having a child, but for adoptive parents who do not have the nine-month gestational period to prepare, this transition may come as a shock. When they get a call about a child who has just been born, or waiting in a foster home, decisions must be made with little time for reflection or second-guessing. I call this the *rapid transition to parenthood.*

Adoptive parents often describe this time as a "whirlwind experience"[6] in which everything in their lives changes, including the nature of the couple's relationship. Yet for many adoptive parents, particularly those who are happily married, this is a good thing. As I mentioned, one of the benefits of being an adoptive parent is that the transition to parenthood generally increases marital satisfaction.[7] While married couples in the general population typically report a small, temporary decline in contentment after childbirth, adoptive parents often find that the transition to parenthood enhances their marriage.[8] Generally, married couples will find that adoption intensifies whatever feelings were present in the marriage beforehand, through what I call the *magnifying effect.*[9] In relationships where significant problems exist, life-cycle transitions such as marriage or having a baby will magnify those problems. On the other hand, in healthy, loving relationships, couples will find that these transitions increase the happiness and satisfaction already felt.

It is worth pointing out that adoptive couples are somewhat "self-selected," in that they have endured challenges such as infertility, thereby strengthening the stability of their relationship. Moreover adoptive parents theoretically are screened by social workers to ensure they are capable of providing a good home to a child, and thus more likely than married parents in the general population to have strong, healthy marriages. When couples such as this realize the fulfillment of their desire to have a child through adoption, there is likely to be a positive outcome.

In addition to changes in the quality of the marriage, a family's social relationships will also evolve—and again, usually for the better. Many couples who experience infertility report feeling as though they are lagging when friends and others in their social sphere become pregnant and begin to have children. As friends increasingly shift their time and interest to childrearing, couples without children feel disconnected. The day-to-day reality of how other couples now occupy their time—changing diapers, supervising homework assignments, or providing late night feedings—seems alien and difficult to relate to. However, because adoption can mean the arrival of a child so quickly, adoptive couples are accelerated back into the fold. I refer to this rapid social transition as *leap-frogging*. This is a critical point when clinical issues may arise, and a good time to seek therapy, if you have not done so already. Having an adoption-savvy therapist to help guide you and your spouse through those changes can be a tremendous asset during these first few months of transition.

With both adopted children and adoptive parents, the ongoing nature of development lends itself to complexity. As I note in an article currently under review

While adoption issues are always present, there are predictable times in an adoptee's life when therapeutic issues related to adoption will wax and wane to greater and lesser degrees over the lifecycle. As we have seen, the teen years, when identity development is so critical is one of those times where adoption saliency emerges in the individual life course.[10]

Figure 9.1 is a graphic description that combines concepts described in narrative by the clinical psychologist David Brodzinski and his colleagues at Rutgers University. It illustrates what Brodzinsky refers to as "adoption salience," the level of importance a child's adoption plays in his life at any given stage of development. [11]

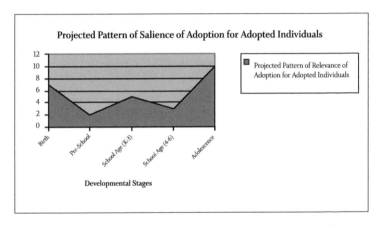

FIGURE 9.1 Projected pattern of salience of adoption for adopted children

As depicted above, average adoption salience rises and wanes at key developmental stages. Adoption salience is high at birth. As it begins to drop in the infant years, the quality of care, the number of foster placements prior to adoptive placement, and

---

* Figures 9.1, 9.2, and 9.3 originally appeared in *Coming Out of the Adoptive Closet* by Kyle N. Weir. Copyright © 2003. Used by permission of University Press of America.

the type of attachment a child forms with parents influence the relevance of adoption issues. When the adopted child enters toddlerhood and preschool—assuming that adoptive placement has occurred prior to age three years—the salience of adoption declines even further but does not altogether disappear. The focus shifts from adoption-related issues to those of academic growth and fine and gross motor development.

Often when the adopted child enters kindergarten and the first years of elementary school adoption salience increases due to new opportunities for socialization. Friends at school begin to ask questions like "Who's your real mommy?" Adopted children are confused by this question because, until now, experience has led them to believe that their adopted parents are their real parents. Assignments by teachers in these early grades often incorporate curriculum about genealogy and family origin, requiring children to bring in baby pictures and family memorabilia. Working through these activities, children and parents revisit the adoption story and must reframe the experience in a social and academic context. Generally, this is resolved in these first years of elementary school, and adoption salience wanes in the later grades of elementary school as children start to focus more attention on academic and extracurricular tasks.

According to the developmental psychologist Erik Erikson, school-aged children go through a developmental stage called "industry vs. inferiority."[12] In the elementary and early middle school years children focus on learning new things and enhancing self-discipline, foregoing pleasure in an effort to prove they can be productive. As Eriksonian industry vs. inferiority stage tasks are being mastered, the adopted child places greater emphasis on reading, mathematics, and overall scholastic performance than the historical fact of their adoption. Thus adoption saliency declines.

However, once the child reaches adolescence, adoption saliency begins to rise dramatically. Identity issues are core issues in both adoption and adolescent development, and the convergence of these two forces contributes to a profound shift in saliency during the teenage years. As the adopted adolescent strives to define her individual identity, her origins and early adoption experiences cannot be ignored. Puberty and reproductive development prompt the teenager to ponder biological origins and contemplate how adoption has affected her life. If adoptive parents fail to respond appropriately to the teenager's rekindled interest in adoption, the adoptee may struggle with unresolved identity issues and confront emotional disturbances, not easily remedied. Parents who are open to discussing the teen's feelings about adoption, often repeatedly and at length, will find these issues easier to resolve.

Figure 9.2 illustrates responses from adoptive parents regarding adoption saliency at different stages across the family development life cycle. In this context, saliency measures the relevance of adoption to the family system across the life-course.

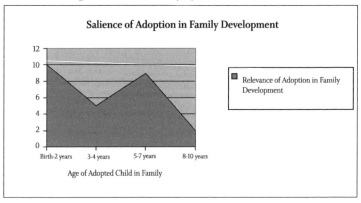

FIGURE 9.2 Salience of adoption in family development

Adoptive parents will often describe adoption as highly relevant in a child's life from birth through the age of two. The family and their social networks frequently discuss adoption as a topic of conversation, and the family regularly attends adoption agency trainings, baby showers, and other adoption-related activities—all indicating a high level of saliency. Adoption salience declines when the adopted child is three to four years old, as parents increasingly focus their attention on the child's abilities, preschool performance, and normative age-related tasks.

As revealed in Figure 9.1, by the time the child reaches five to seven years old, adoption salience begins another upswing. Families have more discussions regarding adoption and their child's understanding of adoption becomes more sophisticated. Partly because of the need to address adoption–related issues with classroom teachers, families become more fluent in talking about adoption. Once their adopted child reaches eight to ten years old, however, the trend reverses. Parents emphasize that normative Eriksonian industry vs. inferiority tasks trump adoption issues during this period. One adoptive mother, Melanie Steward, expressed the diminishing significance of adoption in this way:

> I think after a while, you start living your life. And it becomes about little league and the music class. It becomes about life and not the adoption process so much. Once you kinda get that behind you, you get caught up on life. I'm a private limousine service for my children. It's about living. So if it doesn't come up, it's because it's not pertinent to anything we're dealing with at that particular moment.

As the sample for my dissertation study was limited to adopted children age ten or younger, I devised a set of research questions asking parents to project what degree of salience they anticipated during the child's teenage years. Somewhat surprisingly, parents underestimated adoption salience, reporting that adoption issues were already settled, that problems of identity had been thoroughly discussed, and that as the child's parents they did not anticipate future concerns. Many parents described adoption disclosure as a singular event rather than an ongoing process. This misconception could be due to the fact that parents were currently in a period when adoption saliency was low, and thus they hadn't experienced the teen's rise in adoption saliency. In any case, the parental perception is at odds with what other studies have determined to be a time when the adoption experience is highly important in a child's life.

So why the discrepancy? To answer that question, we need to look at points of divergence in family and individual salience across the life cycle. Notice the pattern of salience in the graph presented in Figure 9.3. In the early years there appears to be a synchronous flow of individual and family development. Both development cycles show adoption saliency high during the child's infancy, declining during the toddler years, reemerging during the early school age years, and diminishing once again during the later elementary school years. However there is a key divergence in the adolescent years. Projections show that for the first time we see a disjuncture or asynchronous flow between individual and family development. Adoptive parents feel like adoption-related issues have already been resolved, while adopted teens are seeking to resurrect undetermined aspects of their adoptive experience—particularly as these issues relate to identity. This disjuncture or period of *asynchronous development*[*] between individual and family development may be a key developmental predictor warranting clinical attention.

---

[*] Asynchronous development usually refers to elements of development occurring at different times or in various levels of progression. Most of the research literature focuses on asynchronous development within the individual—for example, when a child is very cognitively or intellectually advanced, but social-emotional development is delayed. Sometimes preschool-aged children may be cognitively advanced, but their language development is delayed, causing frustration and acting out behaviors (e.g., biting). Here, I'm expanding the concept of asynchronous development to refer to variations in adoption salience between the individual adoptee and his parents. If a teen is struggling with identity-related aspects of his adoption and parents either presume the identity issues are resolved or are unwilling to revisit such issues, the child may develop behavioral and relational conflicts. This may explain why adopted teens often need to come

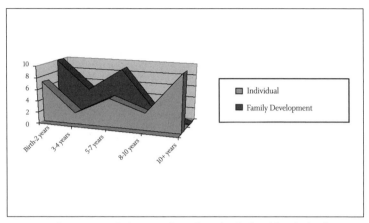

FIGURE 9.3 Comparison of adoption salience by individual and family development

When it comes to issues of adoption salience, the teenage years are critical. Because individual and family development needs are synchronous in the first ten years of the adopted child's life, families are able to avoid or minimize many adoption-related issues. Adoptive parents who have seen their own concerns reflected in concerns of their children come to perceive the "adoption conversation" as a singular event, rather than an evolving process. That view, while founded on reasonable assumptions, ignores the teen's quest for identity forma-

---

into therapy. By comparing points of discrepancy between individual adoptees' developmental needs and the needs of the family system, we may be able to determine when and why families require therapy. This model also helps us better understand how to address the underlying processes leading to undesirable behavior. Therapists treating adoptive families should examine the possible individual-familial asynchronous development patterns, with an eye for points of disjuncture that may be causing clinical difficulties requiring professional services. birth mothers who select childrearing rather than adoption tend to be ignored by parents, who focus their efforts on helping the new baby. By neglecting their teen child these parents fail to finish the job of nurturing their daughter's emotional needs. As a result the teen mother's development is stunted, and she is much less likely to finish her education and later marry.

tion. In reality, teenagers often take years to fully reconcile their identity dimensions. That period of adolescence is fraught with insecurities, doubts, experimentation, differentiation, individuation, and a number of other psychic dilemmas. Adopted teenagers are likely to ask question after question about their heritage, family, and genetic history, particularly where information may be limited or not forthcoming, making it harder for them to figure out who they are.

The bottom line is that no one conversation will encapsulate everything a child needs to know about adoption or themselves, and adoptive families will need to adjust and enrich the conversation as developmental forces require. This is where the "No Less/No More" principle can be a powerful tool.

The No Less/No More Principle

Like learning a foreign language, the adoption experience requires the apprehension of a significant amount of new and unfamiliar information. This can be overwhelming for a child to digest all at once, especially if there are disconcerting facts about the adoption experience or birth family (there was a rape, a birth parent is in jail, there was abuse, etc.) that need to be addressed in a developmentally sensitive way. Parents need to be careful about when and how to present this information (notice I didn't say "if"—family secrets almost always have a way of getting out eventually, and the information needs to be told). The key is to give the child just enough of the story, enough for what the child is prepared for, but not so much that the child will be alarmed or traumatized. Disturbing information that requires a high maturity level to fully understand is best saved until the child is much older. As a veteran therapist, I will tell you there are no simple recipes spelling out when and how you need to talk to your child about adoption. Each child is different and the nature and amount of information you have available may vary. You simply have to let your child's development and ability to understand be the guide.

Try to be open about the fact of adoption from day one. As soon as an infant or older adopted child is placed in your home, make an effort to stress how grateful you are to bring the child into your life. Highlighting adoption at placement will get you into the habit of regularly and frequently talking to the child about adoption long before the child has the cognitive skills to understand what adoption means. As the child grows up, this early investment will ensure that the adoption is seen through an affirming lens that honors and embraces the experience.

In their preschool years, adopted children will often parrot parents, saying, "I a dopted," as if being a "dopted" was a noun. Usually by the time they enter kindergarten, children will begin to ask questions. When your child inquires about adoption, or begins to explore other sensitive topics like human sexuality, try to obey the No Less/No More principle. Essentially, that means answering the child's questions openly and honestly as they are presented. Make sure to answer the question fully. To answer less than what is asked conveys to children that they shouldn't ask in the future or that there is something taboo, secret, or wrong about the adoption experience. But be careful to show discretion when it comes to revealing details of the past. To answer with more than the child is ready to hear will only confuse and overwhelm her, or simply bore her and dissuade future questions. Either way—saying too much or too little—closes the door to future conversations, jeopardizing your ability to recognize and correct distortions in your child's conception of adoption.

Children's books are useful tools to aid in the adoption conversation. I have provided several good books in the resources section in the appendix. Here I'd like to mention Jamie Lee Curtis's *Tell Me Again About the Night I was Born* to illustrate the principle of *disclosure to the child*. The story follows the natural curiosities of a little girl who asks her parents to tell her the story of her adoption. The girl is holding a picture book, which obviously—at least obviously to a parent—contains information about her adoption. She revisits her adoption story by asking for the story to be retold:

> Tell me again how the phone rang in the middle of the night and they told you I was born. Tell me again how you screamed. Tell me again how you called Granny and Grandpa right away, but they didn't hear the phone because they were sleeping like logs.[13]

As the child continues to ask questions, she divulges her adoption story, obviously very familiar to her. With just three words, "Tell me again," Curtis lets the reader understand that the girl's adoption story has been told, over and over, to the point that the story is an integrated part of the child's life. I read this book periodically with my children as a gateway into their adoption story, and I recommend this strategy for other adoptive parents. Reading children's books and connecting the themes to events and people in the child's life is a healthy model for making adoption an open point of discussion.

Once the child matures from preschool and the early grades into the later years of elementary school and beyond, the level of sophistication in the adoption discussion needs to evolve. Because adoption experiences and human sexuality are linked, a child's ability to fully understand their adoption experience is contingent on the ability to understand human sexuality and reproduction. Sometimes as children mature and are better able to understand human sexuality, they develop erroneous ideas about their adoption experience. The euphemism that a birth mother "couldn't take care" of a child may suffice when the child is five or six but must be elaborated on when the child is a teenager. If the child was placed for adoption as a young teen, the explanation may involve discussions about abstinence, birth control, or whatever else the parent deems to be responsible sexual behavior. These same sorts of discussions could also involve disclosures of child abuse, substance abuse, and other delicate topics the maturing child is ready for. The most important thing is that information is revealed gradually at the time parents deem it appropriate for their child to understand and incorporate into his personal history.

As an adoptive parent, you must be particularly sensitive to the issue of identity when your child is a teen. Make sure the teen doesn't identify with the birth parent when you provide painful or disconcerting information, as this may alienate you from your son or daughter. Above all, realize that as children mature, they will get emerging ideas about themselves, their adoption experience, and their identity. Undoubtedly, many of those ideas will be distorted and erroneous—what teenager doesn't have some quixotic ideas? That is why the discussion of adoption needs to be a lifelong process. As social and cognitive skills develop in the maturing child, so will new questions and ideas, and with them, the need to reframe the conversation.

Mismatched Temperaments

Adoptive parents generally do not come in to therapy asking for help with mismatched temperaments between themselves and their adopted children. Instead they come in and describe a child's behaviors, particularly behaviors they do not understand. Often I hear some version of the following: "I don't get Sophia. She doesn't seem to think or behave in normal ways. I've never seen a kid in my family behave that way." After a little prompting, they go on to describe a behavior that is not that extraordinary, but different from how the parent was brought up, and at odds with how parents expect the child to behave. While these behaviors often have their origin in disrupted attachment, they may also be rooted in a related matter—what scholars in the field like to call "goodness-of-fit" or "matched/mismatched temperaments."[14]

But let's take a step back for a moment because we can't talk about mismatched temperaments without a basic understanding of the relationship between nature and nurture. Research shows that the two are inextricably linked, reinforcing and correcting one another constantly, like an ensemble of jazz musicians playing the same piece of music but responding instantaneously to deviations from the score. Although families carry certain genes that predispose children to certain behaviors, a parent's genetic code does not determine the child's life course. It only influences behavior. Most genetic heritability rates are low and other factors such as psychological and environmental conditions are part of the mix, determining whether hardwired preferences manifest or *fail to* manifest certain behaviors.

Here's where it gets tricky. When a child displays certain traits, family members are likely to respond to those traits in kind. That is how traits *do* or *do not* become entrenched behaviors and personality characteristics. For example, our daughter Samantha seems predisposed to be an early riser, having inherited the genetic trait for this sleep pattern from her birth family.[15] On Saturdays, when the rest of the family prefers to sleep in, Samantha is annoyed that no one wants to wake up and play with her. Her response, particularly on "sleeping in days," is to wake up siblings, my wife, and me, not always gently. One morning we heard her down the hall waking up the other children at 4:00 AM, gleefully declaring, "Let's have a party!" Our family's response has varied. Some siblings have adapted to Samantha's sleep cycle and wake up with her routinely, knowing they can get away with mischief before my wife and I are awake to catch them. Other siblings have ignored her,

---

* For a fascinating study linking sleep patterns to individual genetic traits see the work of Hans Van Dongen and his colleagues at the Sleep and Performance Research Center at Washington State University, Spokane. Their article (Tucker, A., Dinges, D. & Van Dongen, H., 2007) in the *Journal of Sleep Research* makes a compelling argument that sleep pattern variability is most likely linked to genetic heritability.

locked their doors, grumbled in anger, and butted heads with her about waking them up. As parents we first tried explaining to her that it was inappropriate for her to wake us up, instituting some basic ground rules to help in the process. We set time limits with her, praised her on the rare times she had slept in, and eventually resorted to identifying sections of the house where she could play as long as she did not disturb others. All of this had limited effectiveness early on, but after years of consistency, Samantha now seems to be able to go to another part of the house and entertain herself with her brother Jason, also an early riser, without disturbing those who wish to sleep in. So although Samantha's sleeping schedule has roots in genetics, it also has evolved in response to the family's reaction.

You might wonder why this is so important to adoption, specifically. Don't children in biologically constructed families have different traits and temperaments than their parents? The simple answer is, yes, but not to the extent or variation seen in adoption. Because adoptive couples possess different genetic material than the children they adopt, they may have traits and temperaments that differ in important ways from adopted children. Adoptive parents, for instance, tend to have higher levels of education, higher IQs, higher socio-economic status, and greater marital stability than the biological parents of their adopted children.[16] Some variation does not matter much, but when there is considerable variation there may be a mismatch in temperament.

According to the researchers David Brodzinksky and Marshall Schechter, the goal in finding placement should be to minimize the mismatch of temperaments between parents and children to produce a "goodness-of-fit."[17] This is a worthy goal, although in reality it may be hard to determine a child's compatibility with the family before placement occurs. Problems with mismatched temperaments are generally discovered after placement but before the adoption is legally finalized. At that point either the mismatch is resolved, usually with the help of a social worker or therapist, or the adoption is at greater risk for later problems. Below Brodzinsky and Schechter illuminate the importance of sustained compatibility between adoptive parents and their children, according to goodness-of-fit:

> When infants are raised by parents who understand them and are sensitive to their needs, development will be optimized. When parents are not able to accommodate to the needs of their children, mismatch problems can occur. Although parental sensitivity is a key determinant, compatibility is viewed as a joint product of the characteristics of the child, the characteristics of the parents, and the family's social situation. . . .The characteristics of parents or children are not static; both change in dynamic responsiveness to each other. . .Goodness-of-fit, then, involves both the family members' ability to attain this state and retain it through dynamic interaction over time.[18]

As part of my clinical work as a therapist, I try to normalize temperamental variation in adoptive families. Like married couples who have genetic differences in mood and personality yet are able to reconcile these to make their marriage work, adoptive parents and children can work through mismatches successfully. It takes a little more work than in their biologically constructed family counterparts, but mismatched adoptive families can become compatible with support.

Sometimes families have a mix of biological and adopted children. These mixed families, one research team notes, have a particularly challenging job.[19] Not only do they need to recognize temperament differences between their adopted and biological children, but they also must exercise caution in monitoring the signals they send to each group. The greater similarity parents have with biological children, with respect to disposition, may lead to real or perceived disparities in how children are nurtured. Interestingly, the researchers found that, despite these differences, adopted children in families with both biological and adopted children tended to do better in terms of adjustment than in families with only adopted children. The study showed that living in a mixed family environment did not harm the biological children, and in fact, had positive effects on the adopted children in the home. It appears that while differences do exist, they are not insurmountable.

Other Developmental Factors to Consider

Throughout this book, I've discussed how factors such as age of placement, attachment pattern history, parental care history, and a child's number of placements affect outcomes for adopted children. In a manner of speaking, all of these factors are developmental in nature. Anything that happens to a child in the history of her life course will affect development, so it is critical to have all the facts in front of you.

If you are sitting in a Team Decision-Making Meeting (TDM) where social workers and other professionals are describing a child you are considering adopting, you'll want to know if there are any developmental delays (i.e., did the child learn to walk, speak, or read in the normal developmental ranges?) Certainly, you'll want to know if any early intervention needs exist and what services should be offered for a child.

Our youngest child, Danny, was born about six weeks prematurely. In cases such as this professionals in the medical and child development fields distinguish between a child's actual age and his *adjusted age*—or the age based on the child's due date. So although Danny was actually seven months old at the time of adoption, his adjusted age was five-and-a-half months. Because of his premature birth, Danny qualified for early intervention services. A child developmental specialist came to our home a couple times a month to teach us developmental exercises, and we also participated in a class at school he and I attended with children like Danny who had minor developmental delays. As a result of these services and our work with him at home, Danny has caught up with many of his peers. In fact, at the time this book was being written, he was either on track or showing advanced proficiency in every major component of developmental assessment. If you are considering adopting a child with developmental delays, be sure to report the child's adjusted age in applying for early intervention services; it could be a deciding factor in the child's eligibility for much-needed support.

Development is a lifelong process and its relevance as a model does not end when the adopted child matures into adulthood. Adoptees in young adulthood may frequently consider searching for and having reunions with their birth family. If the adoptee marries and has children, they may begin a re-examination of their adoption experience, reflecting on events from childhood. Some adoptees have said holding their firstborn child is a unique life experience because it may be the first time they remember meeting a blood relative.

Understanding and applying a developmental model is critical to proper treatment of contemporary adoptive families. As therapists, we often find that historical aspects of the adoption such as age of placement, history of abuse or neglect, or involvement in orphanages or child welfare systems significantly affects a child's development. The complex intersection between individual human development and family development leads to important clinical and relational issues that must be addressed across the life cycle.

Summary

Human development affects every member of the adoption triad. Birth parents who are young and need to mature in order to become effective parents have developmental needs that can best be served through choosing adoption for their child. Adoptive couples also benefit in many ways through the process of adopting, including increasing their marital satisfaction when they adopt. Often these couples experience a whirlwind of lifestyle adjustments as they make the rapid transition to parenthood. Adopted children will find that adoption saliency rises and wanes throughout the life course and is particularly strong in the teenage years.

When we compare periods of adoption salience to family developmental patterns we see moments of synchronous and asynchronous development. Therapists and social workers can be particularly helpful in noting asynchronous points of disjuncture when therapy may be an important tool to reconcile conflicting views parents and children may have about adoption. On top of that therapists may assist parents in establishing an open and ongoing dialogue about adoption, rather than treating the adoption conversation as a singular event. One useful tool in establishing this conversation is the No Less/No More principle, in which the child's evolving level of understanding about adoption forms the basis for progressively more explicit discussions. In addition to helping with asynchronous development concerns, therapists may also provide assistance in addressing mismatched temperaments that arise due to genetic differences between parents and adopted children. Most important, when considering adoption of a child born prematurely or with developmental delays, parents should seek professional services for assistance.

Chapter Ten
Post-Adoption Therapy Services

Several appropriate therapy models are useful in working with adoptive families in treatment. Although I don't claim these models have been researched and verified with the same level of empirical scrutiny demanded by the social sciences, they are reliable "tried-and-true" methods in which you can feel confident. Unfortunately, therapy is a field where fringe elements and gimmicky theories sometimes take hold. One early form of therapy, crawling therapy, suggested that young children who skipped the developmental milestone of crawling and went straight into walking would experience emotional delays. Crawling does help young children learn to read due to the bilateral brain stimulation required as children attempt to visually track their alternating hand movement.* However there is little, if any, evidence that having adults crawl around on the floor will help them deal with their emotional difficulties. You can be certain that the following theories are not in that category. Each is a widely practiced method for helping adoptive families. At different times in my career, I've borrowed elements of each these approaches, and I feel com-

---

* Established therapies like Eye Movement Desensitization and Reprocessing (EMDR) also involve bilateral stimulation of both hemispheres of the brain. A therapist uses tracking with both eyes while discussing emotionally laden issues.

fortable recommending them to you and your family.

There are several litmus tests we may use to judge theo-ries of therapy. Karl Tomm, a professor of psychiatry at the University of Calgary and director of the Family Therapy Pro-gram, developed what he called "ethical postures."[1] Within this framework, he posits that family therapy theories can be judged by several key criteria; namely, whether the therapist (1) reduces or expands a client's options, (2) increases or restricts the client's consciousness of how change occurs in their family system, (3) shares or remains discretionary in revealing knowl-edge, and finally, (4) takes a decisive or measured stance when offering counsel. Therapists choose from among these ethical postures for various reasons such as the needs of the clients, the therapist's personal philosophy, and the model of train-ing available to the therapist in his education or workplace. I have found the most succinct way of conceptualizing marriage and family therapy theories is along the continuum of action versus meaning. Theories that emphasize action or change are not intended so much to help the clients understand or gain insight into why they have difficulties as much as they are to help them eliminate these problems from their life. "Meaning-Based" theories tend to focus, instead, on helping the client gain awareness and understanding about the latent psycho-logical significance of family issues. Although it is presumed behavioral change will follow, such change is not the primary goal of methods on this end of the continuum.

The theories presented in this chapter span the action/meaning continuum. Some are very directive, active, and intent on producing change. Others seek to promote in-sight and reflection into the deeper psychology motivating behavior. Because of the diversity of issues adoption presents to families, it is important to find a theory that reflects your family's particular needs and preferences. Briefly, I should re-mind you that paying for therapy for your child may come from different sources. If you have your own health insurance plan that also covers mental health needs, you likely will be able to find a therapist or provider in your plan who can meet your needs. Additionally, you may qualify for the Federal Title IV-E Adoption Assistance Program (AAP) mentioned earlier in this book.[2] * AAP is a federally funded stipend and health insurance plan given to families who adopt a child determined to have special needs or a history of abuse and neglect. Often therapy services can be accounted for either through the AAP stipend or the government provided insurance plan that accompanies the stipend. Finally, the county or state Child Protective Services agency in your community may provide post-adoption services (e.g., support groups, parent education and training, and other similar programs) that may meet your needs. These agencies are often a good point of contact to find assistance. Later in this chapter, as well as in the appendix, I list additional resources where you can find a therapist to assist you.

Child-Centered Play Therapy

Child-centered play therapy (CCPT) is probably the most commonly used method of play therapy in the United States. Most therapists who advertise that they do play therapy do some type of CCPT. This model emphasizes the humanistic aspects of Carl Rogers's client-centered therapy, begun in the mid-

---

* To receive a $2,000 nonrecurring benefit, the child must be determined to have special needs. This includes (1) unfit parents, (2) a factor or condition such as ethnic background, age, membership in a sibling group, or a medical, physical, or emotional handicap that qualifies the child as having special needs, and (3) an unsuccessful attempt to place the child without Federal Title IV-E adoption assistance. To receive recurring adoption assistance, there are additional requirements. See the Child Welfare Information Gateway's website at http://www.childwelfare.gov/pubs/f_subsid.cfm for more details.

twentieth century, in which the client directs the progress of the therapy while the therapist tries to reflect the client's emotional reality in his questions and responses. As a therapeutic strategy for children, the model gained popularity in 1964 when the psychologist Virginia Axline wrote *Dibs in Search of Self*,[3] chronicling her work using play therapy with a withdrawn five-year-old boy, Dibs, who is a source of embarrassment to his accomplished parents. The book's enduring lesson, one of the fundamental tenets of CCPT, is that each child must discover himself at his own pace.

The current widely accepted leader of the CCPT movement is Garry Landreth, founder of the Center for Play Therapy at the University of North Texas. His publications are numerous, but his book *Play Therapy: The Art of Relationships* is probably his most widely read and cited work.[4] Landreth's training and research center draws people from across the country for professional services and education. Apart from its role in providing training for therapists in CCPT, the center provides play therapy for families and maintains a website with annotated summaries of numerous scholarly articles that show an association between play therapy and improved behavioral self-control in children. If you are interested in learning more about CCPT, the Center for Play Therapy website at http://cpt.nut.edu/ is a superb place to start.

According to Karla D. Carmichael, a professor of counselor education at the University of Alabama in Tuscaloosa, the goal of CCPT is to establish

> . . .a therapeutic environment that provides the client with empathy, unconditional positive regard, and genuine concern and feedback. The feedback is provided . . . by reflecting or mirroring what the client is saying back to the client, conveying that the therapist has understood the client. Reflective listening is more than a simple parroting of the client's words. It requires the therapist give voice to the underlying feelings experienced by the client.[5]

Eight main principles govern therapy sessions using CCPT:[6]

1. Establish a warm, friendly relationship
2. Accept the child as is
3. Exercise permissiveness in allowing free expression of feelings
4. Recognize and reflect on feelings leading to insight for child
5. Allow the child to solve his problems / take responsibility for choices
6. Let the child lead (therapist follows the child's direction)
7. Allow the child to progress at his own pace
8. Set minimal limits that will anchor the child to reality

Most CCPT therapists will have an extensive amount of toys for the child to play with during sessions. These may include puppets, games, sand trays, dolls, toy weapons, animals, and other items through which the child may express a wide range of emotions. Toys generally fall into three broad categories: real-life toys such as dolls, puppets, or kitchen sets; toys for acting out aggression such as toy soldiers, aggressive animals, or toy weapons; and toys intended for creative expression and emotional release such as water, sand, or art supplies. The child is allowed to freely choose whatever toys he wants to play with and the therapist deciphers the symbolic expressions of the play. While a therapist does not generalize from a single selection of a toy (i.e., just because a boy picks up and plays with a toy soldier does not mean he's inherently violent), the CCPT play therapist does look for patterns or trends, asks reflective questions at times to discern the meaning the play has to the child, and tries to engage the child in a supportive, nurturing way. Generally, the child is seen individually, without parents in the room, to encourage the child to explore, create, and interact in a natural state without concern for how such play will be viewed by caretakers. The goal is to provide the opportunity for the child's free, unconstrained expression through play.

This model is very useful for adopted children, particularly if the child has experienced trauma or abuse and is struggling with deep emotional wounds. It allows the child to process the pain of the experience in incremental steps and heal at his own pace. Of course Child-Centered Play Therapy has its limitations. If a child has ADHD, he may find the opportunity to select toys too distracting to be helpful. Nor does the therapy fully address relational issues, such as attachment, because the child is seen individually rather than in a family context. Often the limitations of one model can be accommodated for, by integrating other approaches. That's why most good play therapists will have a range of therapeutic models available at their discretion. While I use the CCPT approach in some situations with children, I have moved more toward an attachment-based model when working with foster and adopted children.

Theraplay

Theraplay is a specific type of play therapy that strives to foster attachment between the parents and child. Several years ago I was fortunate to partner with the Theraplay Institute on a research project conducted with adoptive families in our community utilizing this model. Data from the project revealed that using Theraplay even on a brief basis—12 to 15 weeks of sessions—led to significant improvements in intra-family relationships. One couple came in with their two biological daughters, ages seven and two, and their adopted twin boys, age five. The boys, whose birth mother was deceased, were the adoptive mother's nephews. Related by blood, the family was adopting the children to offer them a new home. Unfortunately, after the adoption took place, the father second-guessed the decision, claiming he'd had enough to handle with his girls. These wild boys from his wife's side were not "something" he was invested in. As you can imagine, the sessions were tough going at first. I think the two students I'd assigned to do co-therapy were as overwhelmed as the parents. But gradually the magic of Theraplay began to take effect. After about five sessions the boys were calmer and much more eager to relate to the family. By the end of therapy, the father had changed from a completely uninvolved, non-participant in the children's life to an at least partially invested adult. While he had not come as far as I would have hoped in terms of showing "paternal instincts" toward the boys, he was enjoying his interactions with them. He liked having someone to do "guy things" with, and appreciated the fact that there were two boys he could introduce to his world. He began to see them not as his wife's problem, but as part of his own responsibility.

Theraplay was begun in the late 1960s as part of a Head Start program in Chicago. Ann Jernberg, a clinical psychologist, received a federal grant to provide services to a vast number of children in preschools. She needed a way to reach these children and began by hiring adults who, regardless of their training, were known to have good skills in working with very young children. As part of the orientation process, she taught her newly hired staff methods of interacting with children in ways attuned to their attachment needs. From those beginnings, came a treatment model that is now practiced in the United States and across Europe and Asia. Today, the standards for providing Theraplay treatment are quite high. Practice of Theraplay is reserved for therapists, mental health clinicians, speech pathologists, and other professionals, and certification is required through the Theraplay Institute in Chicago.⁷*

---

* The author wishes to gratefully acknowledge the Theraplay Institute for the use of their trainings, educational material, and Ann Jernberg and Phyllis Booth's book *Theraplay: Helping Parents and Children Build Better Relationships Through Attachment-Based Play* (New York: Jossey-Bass, 1999), which informed the author as he wrote this section.

Theraplay uses fun, safe, engaging play to build more secure attachments in the family and strengthen the parent-child
bond. Parents are taught how to balance the critical dimensions
of attachment building in their relationships, and the therapist
models and then coaches the parents on how to interact with
their child in more attachment savvy ways. Typically, the treatment is used with a population of children from birth to twelve
years old, but is has been adapted to work with teens and even
adults. The treatment modality routinely involves one or two
parents and a pair of co-therapists working with an individual
child, but is has been found to work effectively with groups, in
school classrooms, in private practices with only one therapist,
and in larger family contexts.[8]

On the continuum of action versus meaning, Theraplay
is very much an action-oriented model. It requires the therapist to take a directive position in therapy and use his personal presence or what is called the "self-of-the-therapist"
as the primary instrument of change. The therapist directly
relates to the child through a series of playful activities to
model appropriate adult-child relationships. Then parents,
when they have learned this style of relating, are bridged
into the play and the therapist supports the play indirectly.
Often the therapist has to direct the parents or child in some
aspect of their interaction to facilitate more healthy attachment. Because children with attachment disorders generally
lack skills in relating to people, the Theraplay therapist has
to direct the subtle nuances of the interaction. This directive
posture of the therapist is in contrast to other popular models of play therapy in the United States (e.g., Client-Centered
Play Therapy) that are nondirective and rely on a variety of
toys, puppets, and other specialized play equipment. While
Theraplay therapists do use some materials, they are mostly
household items such as cotton balls, straws, lotion, M&Ms,
and toilet paper that parents will likely have at home with-

out having to make special purchases. The goal is for the therapist to first model the correct use of the household objects through activities and games, and then bridge the parents into the play techniques. After the parents play the games in session with the children, the family goes home and carries on the activities in their home settings as homework. Theraplay allows the family to experience a different way of relating to each other in everyday tasks in the hope that, once rehearsed, the interaction will carry on without the therapist present. As I have previously written, this structured practice of family interaction is crucial for relationship building:

> A relationship has to involve loving, nurturing, tender interactions coupled with engaging fun, attention, interest, and consideration. A child also must learn to listen, follow directions, and know where they fit hierarchically to feel secure. Structure and limit setting help a child feel safe and secure because they know where the boundaries are and they know an adult is looking out for their interests. Lastly, a child has to face and overcome some level of challenge in order to grow. Having some time in sessions where the child (and parents) has to stretch themselves facilitates growth and development.[9]

The Theraplay approach is grounded in four key dimensions of attachment: structure, engagement, nurture, and challenge. Assessing the family's strengths and weaknesses along these four elements and working to achieve a balance of these dimensions is crucial to treatment.

Structure refers to listening and following directions. It involves establishing a clear sense of hierarchy in the parent-child relationship, whereby the parent is in charge and has the responsibility of leadership, decision making, and protection. Any playful activity that puts parents in charge and requires the child to listen and follow directions may be used to structure games, but there are certain games I particularly recommend during session.* I often start out with a simple hand-stacking game where parents and children take turns stacking their hands together, making the stack go up or down quickly or slowly, depending on the wishes of those involved. After having the therapist model the game, I quickly instruct the parents to take charge of the direction and pace of the game to establish their position of leadership in the family.

Another game I play asks parents to direct a blindfolded child to draw a simple picture, usually a house, tree, or car, on a white board. This activity requires the parents to learn to give simple, detailed directions. It helps parents know what the child is capable of and where deficits in the child's cognition may be inhibiting communication. For example, if the parent says, "draw a line to your left," and the young child doesn't know his left from his right, the parent has to rethink the direction, phrasing it in a way the child understands. I often follow up the blindfold game by instructing the parents on how to give simple directions at the child's level of understanding. Parents often will say to a child, "Clean your room!" without giving any further instruction as to what that means. A few minutes later, the parent will return and get frustrated because the child—big surprise—has done nothing. For many children, the directions need to be more specific in order for anything to be accomplished. The parent needs to say, "First, pick up you Hotwheels," and remain in the room until that task is finished. Only then can the next direction be given: "Next let's pick up the crayons and coloring books." As parents play the drawing

---

* For a detailed list of activities with descriptions, I highly recommend professionals obtain the training provided by the Theraplay Institute. Part of their training materials includes lists and descriptions of activities for each dimension. Parents seeking these types of treatments may browse the Theraplay Institute website at www.theraplay.org or contact the organization for a referral to a certified Theraplay therapist in their area.

blindfolded game, they learn to separate larger tasks into a manageable size the child can handle.

Engagement means being attuned to the child, paying attention to her in a close, personal way. The best physical way to demonstrate engagement is through good eye contact, and, as such, most engagement games are designed to promote mutual and consensual interaction through the eyes. One study demonstrated that consensual eye gazing or "consensual engagement" between infants and parents is a key to secure attachment.[10]

Games like "peek-a-boo" and "patty-cake" require parents and children to face each other and engage with eye contact. Though these games may seem juvenile—you may be asking yourself right now how "peek-a-boo" is a form of therapy—they are known to have therapeutic and attachment-building properties. For school-aged and older children, other engagement games I like to use include *mirroring* (where the child and parent face each other and the child replicates the movement of the parents as if they were looking into a mirror), *collaborative balloon volleyball* (the parent and child face each other and team up to keep the balloon up in the air, counting the number of times they hit the balloon), and *popping cheeks* (the parent and child face each other, puff up their cheeks, and take turns gently poking the cheeks to make them "pop" and release air).

But engagement is, of course, more than a series of eye-contact games; it is about the overall attunement of the parent to the child, a level of playfulness that shows the child his parents are operating on his wavelength. Because most children are naturally playful, adults will connect to children much more quickly when they are willing to show some levity, mirroring the child's natural state. A parent can demonstrate attuned engagement through the voice modulation he uses, a willingness to get down on the floor and play at the child's level, or the ability to "let loose" and be silly with a child when appropriate. Attunement also enters in during the other dimensions (e.g., nurturing a "boo-boo" shows that the parent is aware of and attuned to a child's needs), but playful, attentive engagement is one of the best ways to demonstrate attunement.

Nurturing is a key dimension of attachment building. The capacity for tenderness, care, and affection is part of any good relationship, and parents need to take the lead in nurturing their children. For parents who are too rigid or structured, the Theraplay therapist may have to spend time modeling appropriate behavior. Parents of one family seen in our student-training clinic at the Fresno Family Counseling Center came in afraid to hug their daughter. The child had reactive attachment disorder (RAD) and wanted to hug anyone and everyone constantly, however the parents had limited the child to one hug a day, which wasn't enough to fulfill her needs. Worse still, the daily hug felt wooden and stiff. Through Theraplay, a group of students helped the family show appropriate affection toward their child, using games that involved feeding the child M&Ms and applying lotion to her hands when they were dry. There was still a need for the child to restrain her desire for constant physical affection, but unlike before, limits were based on relationship proximity—i.e., "Don't hug the mailman, save hugs for your mother, father, or siblings." Once the child learned to apply that clear standard, the family could relate to each other in a more naturally tender way.

If the Theraplay therapist and parents are attuned, nurturing occurs whenever the child needs it. If the child comes in with a scrape or minor injury, the therapist should immediately engage the child, acknowledge the wound, express concern or sympathy, and see what he can do to ensure the child is comfortable during the play session. If a child is bumped or otherwise injured in session, therapists should likewise acknowledge the hurt and express sympathy. In Theraplay, we will often put a little lotion around the wound, though not directly in it, as a way of nurturing the child. Other times we may feed a child a snack or juice box while the child sits in the parent's lap.

Soothing an upset child, one who has emotional rather than physical wounds, is a crucial part of nurturing. As recent brain research indicates, physical touch from a caregiver to a child helps to deepen bonds of attachment. It is important to point out that, in Theraplay, touch is never used in a coercive way. It is always done in the presence of a parent, with the idea that the therapist models the technique for the parent to apply at home.*

There are several nurturing games and activities I like to use to with families in therapy. One involves parents' feeding M&Ms or another appropriate snack to children. I always check with parents first about allergies, and my rule is that young children are not allowed to feed themselves; the parent must put the M&M in the child's mouth. Other games include *lotioning hands,* which is simply rubbing some lotion on a child's hands and being silly, and *hiding five dots of lotion,* requiring parents to find and rub in five dots of lotion I've applied on the child's body, usually behind the ears, on their elbows, or on the tip of their nose. Nurturing games and activities like these are a vital part of enhancing the attachment between parents and their children.

Challenge is the final dimension of attachment building. Developmental theory teaches us that all people, including children, need to stretch themselves and overcome challenges to grow and develop. Complacency, ease, and mediocrity do not inspire growth, particularly when it comes to deepening bonds of attachment. Instead, attachment is fostered as parents

---

* As a practice, I never see young children alone when using Theraplay. Typically, touching in the clinical context occurs only as part of activities such as pretend face painting and patty-cake, or hugging initiated by the child. Although I never instigate a hug with a child, rejecting a child's appropriate hug runs counter to the type of parent-child attachment Theraplay attempts to foster

and children face and overcome challenges together through collaboration. Some of the games and activities I've previously described may be too easy for the age and maturity level of older elementary school or middle school children. Adding a challenge dimension to an otherwise easy activity makes it more interesting and appropriate for the child. One of my favorite challenge activities is *team cotton ball soccer,* a game in which one parent and child team up across the table from another co-therapist and me, and using straws, we try to blow a cotton ball off our opponents' side of the table. In another popular game, a variation of the relay race called *figure eights around the pillows,* I ask the child run in a figure eight pattern around two pillows on the floor and "high five" the parent waiting at the end; I time them, usually several times, as they try to achieve a faster time. In challenge games, the parent and child bond as they become co-competitors.

I'll never forget my more successful clinical experiences with two brothers living in one of the roughest parts of South Central Los Angeles. The boy's grandmother, who had attained legal guardianship to keep the boys from entering the child welfare system, brought them in to my office because the older brother didn't look out for his little brother. To impress his friends, nine-year-old Jamaal would walk faster than his five-year-old brother, Michael, on their way home from school. Jamaal would laugh when his friends teased Michael, rather than standing up for him. Though it may seem like a small thing, such lack of fraternal care can have devastating consequences in communities with an active gang presence. For reasons one can probably imagine, gangs often prey upon young children without strong family connections. Somehow we had to work with Jamaal to get him to be more protective of his little brother.

One activity I found particularly successful with these boys involved a makeshift basketball game using a racquetball and a small wastepaper basket. The boys would be a team and play two-on-one against me. Whenever they cooperated, sharing the ball and playing well as a team, I would play less defensively and let them be successful. But when they were not collaborating as a team, I made it virtually impossible for them to score. They had to learn to overcome the challenge by working together and helping each other as brothers. This did the trick, not only in sessions, but also in their neighborhood and home environment.

Theraplay is usually done with a therapist, co-therapist, one or two parents, and one child. But because of my adherence to a family-systems perspective, I have clinically worked with much larger family systems than the traditional Theraplay modality specifies. At our university's student training clinic, the Fresno Family Counseling Center, I have begun to partner with the Theraplay Institute to develop an expanded model of Theraplay for adoptive families called Whole Family Theraplay. This model invites all members of the family system to participate in Theraplay sessions. Although it can be easy to give a child one-on-one attention in the attachment-building context of regular Theraplay, clients from families with many children have a hard time implementing Theraplay when they go home and have to deal with the competing needs of multiple children.

Whole Family Theraplay, developed for adoptive families in California's Central Valley, allows Fresno State graduate students earning their master's degree in counseling to work in paired partnerships with adoptive parents and their children. Sessions have included as many as eleven people. (Two co-therapists, two parents, and seven children is the largest Whole Family Theraplay session we have done so far.) In most of the families, at least one of the adopted children struggles with attachment issues. Strained sibling dynamics, competition for parental attention, lack of control over impulses, and attention-deficit/hyperactivity disorder (ADHD) are other common clinical concerns. The presence of four adults instead of two helps calm things down and gives much-needed structure to large family sessions. Once the children and parents buy into the games and activities, families seem to develop an ability to handle the complexity of their dynamics. Parents may learn how to conduct parallel play activities, where each parent and therapist is responsible for only one or two children at any given game. At other times the family may play as a whole group. By varying the activities, families learn to better manage the interactions that occur in large family systems.

One of the principles that laid the groundwork for Whole Family Theraplay derives from the research of Carlfred Broderick, a marriage and family therapist known for his work with married couples. When studying the effect of TV watching on family interaction patterns, Broderick observed that for small families, too much time in front of the television reduced the number of family interactions necessary for healthy family cohesion. However for larger families who already showed high levels of complexity in their interactions, modest amounts of TV watching actually reduced the number of interactions to a manageable level, enhancing the family's sense of connection. 11 Broderick's key point—that the size of a family or group changes the nature of its interactions—is easy to observe in the school setting. With a large number of children and no structured activities, chaos, complaining, and misbehavior are sure to ensue. However if we can get those same children organized in a structured, unidirectional activity, an activity with a single focal point, things will run much smoother.

Adoptive families with a large number of children often come into our program complaining of negative family interactions. We hear complaints about sibling arguments, a particularly "bad child" who was the scapegoat of the family's ills, or a child not living up to behavioral expectations set by the parents. Reasons parents give for this bad behavior are fairly typical: attachment issues, ADHD, and so on. These are important, but often the reason the family becomes overwhelmed is because they lack structuring mechanisms to reduce the complexity of large family interactions.* Whole Family Theraplay not only addresses the clinical issues, but also guides the family through playful activities that regulate the sorts of interactions parents have with their children. During a session we may have the family play Mother-May-I or Red-Light/Green-Light as a demonstration of how all family members can be involved in a single activity, at one time. If an activity requires more individualized, personal attention—for instance, teaching parents how to nurture a young child though feeding—the family must learn about taking turns, parallel play, and pacing. This enables children to trust that everyone's needs are met inside the family, even if not immediately. They learn to exercise patience.

Apart from the benefits of structured play, I have found Theraplay to be useful because of its adaptations for the high numbers of abused and traumatized children who enter into adoptive and foster families. When it comes to working with these children practitioners are trained in several areas: how to calm a child in a state of heightened arousal; how to foster a child's trust in his new caretakers; how to use touch in a safe, soothing way. Most importantly, therapists work to restore a child's damaged faith in adults so he may come to accept his adoptive or foster parents.

Theraplay has revolutionized how I work with children, particularly adoptive and foster children, by redirecting the focus of my treatment to the attachment issues seen in many of these children. Unlike other therapeutic models that focus

*"Large" has been cleverly described by my former professor Marcia Laswell as "anything more than four kids [when] the two parents run out of hands to hold onto children."

strictly on technique, Theraplay assists parents in being pro-active about learning a "style" of interaction in the relation-ships they forge with their children. Theraplay is less about mastery of a specific technique or activity than it is about fos-tering better relationships. For clinicians working with fami-lies inside the public child welfare systems, it is one of the most powerful approaches to treatment currently available. As a child's attachment issues are addressed in structured ac-tivity, distracting and confrontational behaviors will in most cases improve.

Dyadic Developmental Psychotherapy

Dyadic Developmental Psychotherapy (DDP) was created by Daniel Hughes, a clinical psychologist who for many years has provided therapy to adopted and foster children. Like Thera-play, DDP is based in attachment theory and relies on play ac-tivities to build attachment. But to some extent, DDP is more inclusive of a child's language than Theraplay. It stresses the importance of attunement of the therapist to the child, and uses both verbal and non-verbal methods to foster this connec-tion. If a child expresses sadness, the therapist makes a state-ment in a tone of voice congruent with that sadness, acknowl-edging the child's grief. At the same time the therapist tries to match the child's facial expressions and non-verbal gestures, further reflecting the child's vantage point. Thus DDP strikes a balance between action and meaning: seeking both behavioral change, and insight into the child's thoughts and feelings.

   In his excellent book *Attachment-Focused Family Therapy,* Hughes examines the concept of "intersubjectivity," the suc-cessful merging of attention and understanding between a parent and her child.[12] According to Hughes, intersubjectivity takes place whenever the parent and child engage in the coop-erative construction of meaning. Consider, for instance, when a parent reads a children's book to her son or daughter: the child's full understanding of the book is dependent on the parent's questions and clues, her corrections and affirmations. Or as Hughes writes:

> I am referring to those moments when the parent and child are in synch: when they are affectively and cognitively present to each other; when the vitality of their affective states are matched; their cognitive focus is on the same event or object; and their intentions are congruent. . . (W)hen two individuals are engaged intersubjectively their affect is being co-regulated and they are co-creating the meaning of the objects or events they are attending to.[13]

The main point is that attachment and intersubjectivity work together in a reciprocal, cooperative—almost symbiotic—relationship. One might sum up Hughes's "intersubjectivity," as the emotions parents and children hold around shared experience. These are as much about the experience itself (intersubjectivity) as they are about the broader context of the relationship (attachment bond).

DDP delineates four central traits to its therapeutic model: playfulness, acceptance, curiosity, and empathy (PACE). For DDP to resonate with the child, *playfulness* in the attitude and stance of the therapist is essential. Equally important, is playfulness between the parent and child. Play is the medium of communication for most children; and in sessions with kids who have been traumatized or otherwise feel unsafe, playfulness puts children at ease, allowing them to feel the sense of safety they need to heal.

> When families come with memories of events associated with shame, fear, and conflict at the forefront of their attention and are motivated to reduce these states, they are not likely to initiate or even be very receptive to experience of joint playfulness. Yet this attitude of playfulness leads infants into states of companionship with their parents from which they co-create the meaning of their world. A playful stance is invariably associated with a sense of safety from which children are ready to reach out to the world again, affectively resonating with it, and coming to understand it

within joint experiences of playful understanding with their parents. If the therapist is able to integrate a playful attitude into the treatment session it will often provide a way to realize that the stressful experiences are only one aspect of the ongoing relationship. They are able to take their place within a coherent family narrative.[14]

When using elements of DDP in therapy, I always remind myself that the private feelings of the child—the subtext—is just as important as the play itself. Often children will whisper to notify me when the play is not going as they had intended. It is as if the formal game or play is the "front stage" and whispering is the playful way that children take me to the "backstage" of child social interaction.[15] Much like at a dinner party when a hosting spouse invites her husband to "help her in the kitchen" after he says something ridiculous or offensive—the invitation being a subtle request for the husband to come into the kitchen to talk about his comments in private—whispered backstage interactions are children's way of being their true selves without pretense. I teach my students to pay close attention whenever a child whispers in play therapy sessions. And this is a lesson for parents, too: A child tends to speak volumes when he whispers.

Applied to DDP, *acceptance* has multiple meanings.[16] In part, it refers to a therapist's ability to conform to the rhythms, patterns, processes, and behaviors of the family. This type of attunement allows the family and therapist to feel comfortable with one another and aids the therapist in understanding the family's needs. Acceptance also implies a high level of commitment and "unconditional positive regard" as a therapeutic stance.[17] According to Hughes, acceptance is closely connected to an individual's feeling of personal security:

> Most of us, within our developing attachment relationships, hope deeply that we will be accepted as we are... Acceptance communicates a commitment to the person and a confidence in who that person is. Without a sense of acceptance, fears of rejection and abandonment are not too far from awareness. Acceptance sees

under the behavior and communicates that the relationship will remain regardless of the conflicts and separations.[18]

Particularly for adopted children and their families, acceptance helps reduce the shame, anger, and discouragement that sometimes surface when a child's history is filled with abusive and traumatizing events. Deep-seated and terribly distressing inner turmoil often underlies the behavioral problems of the child. That needs to be addressed for the child to successfully assimilate into the new family. When the child feels accepted and understood, those negative feelings become less dominant and the child is more likely to display desirable behaviors.

Curiosity is the third therapeutic stance in DDP and an important one. If the therapist remains curious about the family's processes, she will be better able to explore the "presenting and emerging themes" of the family;[19] she will come to know the family, and develop a sense of affection for them. But curiosity is far more than just asking questions at intake. Curiosity involves an intimate knowledge of the adoptive parent and child, a wonder about them that conveys the message that these children are worth knowing and interesting enough to sustain our wonder.

For Hughes, curiosity leads to *empathy,* and in fact the two are interrelated: "Curiosity is the cutting edge of empathy, while empathy leads curiosity to new depths."[20] As the therapist becomes more attuned with and knowledgeable about his client, the therapist's affective states will shift toward empathy. Unlike psychoanalysis, in which the therapist may appear standoffish, DDP requires the therapist to "join," or be intersubjectively connected with the client's feelings and experiences:

> The therapist is led to where she is now standing with her client. She is experiencing an event that her client had previously experienced without her. She is experiencing her client's experience of the event. Her experience is affective and reflective (a/r). Together with her client, she is co-regulating the affect associated with the event and co-creating its meaning. This is empathy.[21]

Once the therapist has become attuned with the client's emotional or affective state, he may explore themes pertinent to the child's experiences, problems, or life-story, while keeping a close watch on the child's reactions.[22] The therapist expects the child to disrupt the process: distressing revelations of personal and familial history, failure to develop stable attachment patterns, trauma exhumed from the past, fluctuations in attitude and comfort level—these are a natural part of the process. The therapist's job is to help the child get past these psychic breaks and disruptions, repairing the relational connections.

As an attachment-based approach to clinical treatment of children, DDP has some similarities to Theraplay, and many of the leading Theraplay therapists and trainers have begun integrating DDP and Theraplay in their clinical work. Both models involve play, both focus on helping parents and children build more secure attachments, and both require a high level of attunement between the therapist and the client. So while there is not a perfect correlation between the two models, there are certainly strong parallels. One key difference is that DDP typically involves a more serious discussion of feelings. In my own work, I have found times when doing Theraplay was enhanced by some of the emotional and cognitive discourse found in the DDP model.[23] By integrating these two models, a therapist has a powerful approach for treating adopted and foster children who have histories of abuse and neglect.

Bear in mind that DDP was born out of the need for a clinical method of psychotherapy to treat foster and adoptive children with serious psychological problems—usually problems stemming from experiences of trauma. Because its theoretical framework arose from the specific concerns of adoptive families, you may find that it resonates well with the needs of you and your family.

Cognitive-Behavioral Therapy (CBT)

Cognitive-behavioral therapy (CBT) is an umbrella term for several models of treatment aimed at correcting unhealthy thought patterns.[24] Though there are significant differences in the various incarnations of CBT, they all tend to work on the same assumption: namely, that people's thought processes affect what they do. While this connection seems obvious enough, applying the principle to the therapeutic setting can lead to interesting discoveries about what drives a child's behavior and how to adjust this behavior by recalibrating patterns of thought. The thinking is that if therapists can change the cognitive assumptions and beliefs that lead to a patient's maladaptive behaviors, then the behaviors themselves will change.

The late Albert Ellis, the originator of cognitive-behavior therapy, is believed to be one of the most influential psychotherapists in the history of the field. Ellis found that people often subscribe to faulty, irrational beliefs, which direct their behaviors in calamitous directions.[25] In the patient's mind, this might sound something like "people must always like me" or "I *need* to be constantly worried because the world is a dangerous, fearsome place." In therapy-speak, we hear this referred to as "catastrophizing," "horriblizing," or over-generalizing a situation—generally to the point where the thinking disrupts behavior.

For children, the behavioral aspects of CBT may be even more relevant than the cognitive portions. Basic behaviorism is based on the work of B.F. Skinner's operant conditioning and holds that behavior can be either reinforced or punished by the consequences one receives for his actions.[26] Therefore, as a parent, if you want a child to clean his room, you might positively reinforce the child by giving him allowance money, candy, verbal praise, or some other similar reward when the job is complete. On the other hand, negative reinforcement for cleaning the room might mean you stop nagging your child once the room is clean. Once the child associates cleaning his room with freedom from nagging, he will likely keep his room clean in the future.

Here's a more personal example. In graduate school, I hated the feeling of being overwhelmed with too many papers to write at the end of each semester. To jumpstart the writing process, I began to use as motivation what I called my "negative relief state," allowing the task of writing papers to bother me early on in the semester. At times the paper writing tasks would feel so oppressive that all I wanted to do was write the papers a month or two early to get them off my back. I found a sense of relief that I quite enjoyed when the papers were written early. While my friends and fellow students were scrambling to get papers done at the last minute, often pulling all-nighters, I basked in the relief of finished work. In this way, self-imposed negative reinforcement helped me overcome my natural inclination to procrastinate. The key for me was to let the tasks bother me early and deeply enough that I wanted to get them done more than anything else. For parents of adopted children, this model may work, too, albeit externally imposed. Allow yourself to stick to a standard you hold important and be consistent with your child. Eventually, he'll see what a relief it is just to get things done to meet that standard.

In Skinner's model, as a corollary to the reward, the absence or presence of punishment also can be used as reinforcement to modify voluntary behavior.* Somewhat counterintuitively, a so-called "positive" punishment would be to add a consequence to a child's undesirable behavior. For example, a

---

* B.F. Skinner used the term "punishment" in operant conditioning, and I repeat the use of the term, here, though I find it distasteful. I normally prefer to use the term "discipline" because discipline implies "to make a disciple of" or to teach, whereas punishment connotes the infliction of pain.

parent might choose to make a child wash the entire family's dirty dishes if he misbehaves at the dinner table. Conversely, negative punishment involves suspending privilege as a consequence of a child's undesirable behavior. That may include grounding a child for a period of time, restricting a child from a specific treat or activity, or placing a child in time-out.* Today, most therapists advocate for negative punishments—loss of privileges, time-outs, restrictions, and so forth—rather than corporeal punishments.

For the average preverbal child, behaviorism in all of its forms (e.g. classic conditioning, operant conditioning) is essential, allowing us to interpret and train cognitive processes that cannot yet be expressed in words. Behaviorism holds that the "mind is a black box," meaning that although we do not know exactly what goes on in the brain, the inputs and outputs of one's thinking are observable in behavior. By studying the behavior of a child, we can improve our ability to predict what he is thinking. When you see a crying infant, you might guess the baby is hungry, tired, or in need of a fresh diaper. In a similar fashion, you can infer children have been abused when they act out sexually or exhibit extreme violence. Generally, parent-training programs in CBT are designed to modify behavior rather than feelings. They show parents how to use external

---

* Timeout is measured as a one-minute discipline period, per infraction, multiplied by the child's age. Afterward there may or may not be a discussion of the misbehavior and desired alternative behavior, depending on which parenting model one is applying. Recently, due to the debate between behavioral approaches and attachment approaches, attachment-oriented therapists have advocated "time-in," rather than "time-out." The thinking is that time-out conveys a message of separation and the undesirability of the child in the parent-child attachment relationship. Time-in involves staying with the child, while reducing the level of activity, engagement, and external stimulation as the parent helps to co-regulate the child's emotions. Those who favor time-out counter that time-in rewards bad behavior because the child receives attention from the parents for his misbehaviors.

motivators such as stickers and charts, monetary rewards, and treats like M&Ms and candy bars.[27] They stress punishment strategies and redirection, rather than deep psychological inquiry. CBT practitioners have always placed a strong numerical emphasis on assessment. Typically, a CBT therapist will suggest journaling as a way to tabulate the baseline frequency of certain behaviors. Some therapists may use a formal evaluation like Beck's Daily Record of Dysfunctional Thoughts. Others suggest that patients keep a notebook, jotting down how frequently they think or behave in a particular way. Along with the journal, CBT therapists often use specific testing instruments to evaluate a child with troubling behaviors or thought patterns. Perhaps best known are the Myers-Briggs Type Indicator, the Minnesota Multiphasic Personality Inventory, and the Beck Depression Inventory, but there are literally hundreds of tests a CBT therapist may appropriately choose. CBT therapists will also use subjective units of distress (SUD) scales, asking clients to attempt to quantify feelings, thoughts, and behaviors on a scale of one to ten. All of this strong numerical emphasis has led to extensive empirical research supporting the effectiveness of behavioral and CBT approaches. That is one of the reasons that CBT, and behaviorism in general, has enjoyed such widespread usage among therapists treating children and adolescents. It also explains, in part, why so many social workers and adoption and foster care workers apply behaviorism in their work with children.

One of the most notable advocates for CBT among adopted and foster children is Richard Barth, a respected scholar, and dean of the School of Social Work at the University of Maryland in Baltimore. Over the last twenty-five years Barth has prolifically expanded the knowledge base within the field of adoptive studies. In a recent article published in *Child and Family Social Work*,[28] Barth and his colleagues argue against attachment-based approaches, suggesting these lack the empirical validity of models rooted in behaviorism. Interestingly, the attachment models the researchers cite are among the most controversial. "Holding therapy" and "rebirthing" are widely considered coercive therapies, and have been rejected by every major reputable mental health professional association. And, to be sure, attachment models cast a wide net. DDP and Theraplay are newer models and still gathering empirical support, such as through my work with the Fresno State Theraplay project, but the research so far indicates that both DDP and Theraplay are safe, effective models of treatment.[29]

During my doctoral internship as a foster family agency social worker, I often applied behavioral approaches with foster and adopted children. Though most children would respond well to behavioral treatments, I noticed that children with attachment disorders often regressed. When parents emphasized behavior, the attachment-disordered child did not respond in kind. In fact, on several occasions, the interaction between the parents and child escalated into heated, inflammatory exchanges, with parents "upping the ante" in terms of consequences as the child became increasingly defiant. Behaviors got worse.

The reality is that children with attachment disorders tend to personalize consequences: they perceive "punishment" as a personal and relational assault, and that perception then destabilizes the child's attachments and leads to problems in the child's emotions, behaviors, and self-perception. However, when attention is paid to attachment, children begin to feel more secure, behaviors improve, and behavioral approaches generally become effective. Due to the prevalence of attachment issues in adoption, it has been my experience that non-coercive attachment therapies tend to be more effective with adoptive families where attachment-disorders are present. Starting with an assumption of improving attachment may truly be the best way of improving behavior rather than initially focusing on behavior itself. Once the relationship improves, then the child may be ready for subsequent behavioral treatments.

Clinically, I have come to believe that behaviorism works with most children, but when attachment problems are present the therapist and parents must temporarily suspend, or at least tamp down, behavioral approaches and focus on helping the child feel more secure in his attachments. If experience is any judge, it is generally best to wait for the relational and familial problems to improve through attachment-based treatment before introducing behavioral therapy. That may take time. But there is no reason that behaviorism and attachment-based strategies need to be viewed as conflicting methods. Rather they may be integrated, quite successfully, into a sequential treatment plan that meets the needs of adopted and foster children.

Narrative Family Therapy

Narrative family therapy is different from most classical treatment approaches and represents a solidly meaning-oriented therapy on the action-meaning continuum. Developed by Australian social worker, Michael White, and New Zealand family therapist and anthropologist, David Epston, the post-modern theory presupposes lives are like a story or narrative that one may revise, reframe, or re-write.[30] This is true for both individual lives and the lives of families. This is also true for client's past, present, and future life story. In a word, narrative family therapy helps clients *restory* their lives.

Core to this approach is the belief that the therapist can help the family make sense of their life. Early in the process, the therapist may help the patient conceptualize their experiences in a different light, make alternative suggestions for the significance of certain events, or challenge the client to confront assumptions about himself that he has yet to critically examine.

Later the therapist attempts to empower families to "write" a new chapter in their lives by making wholesale changes in the way they think, feel, and behave. As part of its mission, this model also draws heavily on social justice advocacy; it seeks to empower marginalized groups to find their voice and challenge oppressive sociological institutions.

According to the researchers Michael Nichols and Richard Schwartz, this model has several goals.[31] One of these is for clients to *externalize the problem*. Rather than allowing blame and infighting among themselves, families are encouraged to pull together against outside threats responsible for many of their problems. Therapists steer clients away from *problem-saturated stories,* replacing them with stories that are more positive and therefore more likely to lead to meaningful change. As new perspectives are co-constructed, therapists may look for *unique outcomes,* or times when the client's presenting problems are not problems, per se, but distortions in thinking. They seek to enhance what was good about those times, ask *relative influence questions* "Who's in charge: the person or the problem?" and work with the patient to build a more self-affirming master narrative. In the literature, this final goal is referred to as *reauthoring the whole story.* Once the new story is introduced therapists will reinforce and enrich its themes, thus strengthening the patient's new way of seeing themselves. All along patients are *deconstructing destructive cultural assumptions*—or challenging oppressive social and cultural conditions that interfere with the patient's well-being.

As you probably noticed, the preceding paragraph is full of specialized terminology. Narrative family therapy is deeply focused on language and the meaning of words. Like gifted literary novelists, narrative therapists choose their words carefully, using phases to draw out new insight, meaning, and perspective into their client's lives. By doing so they hope to increase options available to families, give them new hope, and inspire lifestyle changes that lead to increased self-confidence and optimism. Sometimes the techniques get a little overshadowed by the semantics, but the driving principle behind narrative therapy is simple—help clients see their lives in a new light so they can regain faith in themselves.

Generally, I do not use narrative family therapy, although the few times I have used it, I've had encouraging results. Once in graduate school I worked with an older adopted child who had developed a highly self-critical, pessimistic life narrative. Like many adopted children, he believed that his birth mother had "given him up for adoption" because he was unwanted and unlovable. As proof, he showed me cigarette burn marks and other scars he had received from his birth mother. I found out more of the story from his adoptive parents. The child's birth mother was a friend of the family. Her drug and alcohol problem was debilitating and chronic, and this dependency led to the child's abuse and neglect. After the child was brought in, I began using narrative family therapy to reframe the boy's understanding of the circumstances of his adoption. I talked about how his mother was sick and couldn't care for him; the American Medical Association describes alcoholism as a disease, and I figured this was one appropriate way for him to conceptualize it. When the problem became a function of his mother's illness, not his personal worth, the boy began to respond better to the love and guidance of his new adoptive parents. Eventually, he came to view his mother's illness as a "disease" or "alcoholism," rather than some inner deficiency on his part or the fault of his birth mother.

As I hope I've shown, the emphasis with narrative family therapy isn't always strictly about uncovering what is true. More important is finding out what works to help clients improve their lives. Sometimes the grim reality of the child's adoption circumstances (e.g., the child was born as the result of a rape, or the victim of horrific abuse) can cause serious psychological disturbances while the child's self-esteem and identity formation are still developing. Again, be careful to give the child useful information rather than the whole truth right way. And be sensitive to the developmental needs of your child when disclosing sensitive information. Eventually the truth should come out, but only in a developmentally sensitive way when the child is ready for it.

A couple of years after seeing this client, I was conducting interviews with adoptive parents for an earlier book, *Coming Out of the Adoptive Closet,*[32] when I again encountered the relevance of narrative approaches to adoptive families. Whenever I asked parents to tell me their adoption story, they would take pains to describe how they decided to adopt, how the child was placed in their home, and so on. I never had to explain what I meant by that phrase "adoption story" because parents were naturally inclined to view adoption this way. Parents would talk about whose story it was to tell—and whether or not ownership of the adoption story belonged to the parents or the child. Most insisted the adoption story was the child's story. However the story of the family is equally important—a point I emphasize in my last book:

> The adoptive parents already see the experience as the "child's story." In reality the story belongs to the whole family—each with a different perspective. The child has his or her story, the parents have their story, and the grandparents and extended kin have their version of the story. Each story or perspective needs to be heard. Therapists should consider using narrative techniques with the whole family, not just the child.[33]

Currently, empirical support demonstrating the efficacy of narrative family therapy lags behind what we find for cognitive-behavioral therapy. Still, a growing body of research suggests narrative family therapy is effective,[34] and more conclusive studies could very well increase the popularity of this model in the near future.

Psychoeducational Approaches

Psychoeducational approaches are not considered comprehensive treatments for adopted children and their families, but they are critical adjunctive services to therapy, widely used with adoptive families in two settings: (1) school-based groups and consultations and (2) post-adoption services parent support groups.

School counselors generally do not provide therapy, per se. Their model is to provide brief individual consultations or group counseling sessions for students, and offer referrals to families for the deeper work of family therapy. Generally, the use of psycho-educational counseling in school programs is to provide basic information in a safe environment where the child may ask questions and process their experiences. School psychoeducational programs are likely to cover many of the topics found in this book: identity issues, transracial issues, developmental information, and so on.

Psychoeducational approaches are also useful for teachers, some of whom may be unaware of the anxiety genealogy assignments can provoke in adopted children. Bringing a baby picture to class, making a family tree—these assignments can be a source of distress to such children, for many reasons, yet teachers may not accommodate such concerns without proper training. Many school counselors now provide workshops for faculty and staff in their schools to foster greater sensitivity to adopted children and minimize the risk for hurtful or difficult assignments.

Ecosystemic Play Therapy

One last model of treatment bears discussion. Professor Kevin O'Connor, director of the clinical PhD program and PsyD programs at Alliant International University, in Fresno, is the co-founder of the Association for Play Therapy.* His therapeutic model, ecosystemic play therapy, combines the biological aspect of ecological models with sociology, child psychology, human development, and systems theory. Philosophically, O'Connor views the child as part of a multi-layered environment, a sort of human epicenter where interpersonal, cultural, and organizational systems collide.

Imagine a foster child about to be adopted. How many layers of systems exist around that child? The child's own inner psychology is part of what explains the child's feelings, thoughts, and behaviors. But that child also exists in a family system—in reality, two or more different family systems. The child has connections to his birth parents, siblings, and extended birth family, as well as to the adoptive family and their consanguinity. The child also is surrounded by organizational systems. He has to learn to operate in a school system, the foster care system, and any other systems—sports leagues, Boy Scouts, hobby-oriented groups—in which he is involved. This child also exists within a larger, sociologically derived set of cultural parameters. Does he live in an urban or rural setting? How do race and ethnicity play a role in his life? What gender expectations come to bear? As you can see, ecological systems can get remarkably complex. So how does play therapy help a child be successful at all of these levels?

Well, it is not that simple. Often the first step is restructuring the way the child thinks about these issues. To do that, the therapist attempts to change the systems by interacting with schoolteachers, social workers, foster parents, and other important figures in a child's life. If those critical adults can't enact institutional change, the therapist tries to at least change how the child perceives such systems. For example, if a foster

---

* Kevin O'Connor and Charles Schaefer co-founded the Association for Play Therapy in 1982. The organization is headquartered in Fresno, California, and information about the association can be found on their website at www.a4pt.org.

child is having problems in school, an Individualized Education Program (IEP) might be created to help the child. An IEP is a written description of the child's unique educational needs, designed to help teachers understand the child's disabilities, as well as what modifications might be needed to aid in the learning process. Everyone in the child's system—the school teacher and guidance counselor, the principal, the foster parents, the child's therapist, his social workers, and conceivably every other pertinent professional—all would be invited to an initial planning meeting. An ecosystemic play therapist participating in an IEP might advocate for changes in the classroom such as moving the child's seat, modifying his homework assignments, or giving him extended time on tests. If the teacher is unwilling to make all of the suggested changes, the ecosystemic play therapist generally encourages at least minor modifications, while working with the child on strategies to improve learning. During therapy you might find a therapist "playing school" with the child, or using puppets or toys to represent key people in the school system. Through play and interpretation, the therapist helps the child see new ways of behaving and interacting.

As part of ecosystemic play therapy, developmentally appropriate toys are provided for the child—generally three toys below the child's developmental level, one toy at the appropriate developmental level, one toy above the child's developmental level, and two that represent the child's presenting problem. The toys represent the challenges the child faces inside his ecological systems and are also used to determine a child's developmental level. Below are some of the toys you might see used in ecosystemic play therapy:

- Level I (ages 0 to 2 years: sensory play—baby bottle, blanket, stuffed animals, large ball, attention getters)
- Level II (ages 3 to 6 years: pretend play—drawing materials,

paints, dress-up costumes)
- Level III (ages 6 to 11 years: projective play—miniature people, houses, cars, dolls, school, and hospital)
- Level IV (ages 11 to 12 years: constructive play—art, construction sets, model kits, sand tray)

The purposes of such careful developmental attention are threefold:

- To help assess where the child is emotionally (a ten-year-old child who consistently chooses to play with toy material from Level II probably has significant delays)
- To help children mature, heal, and grow through the type of play most appropriate for their age
- To provide occasions for symbolic play (sometimes called "representational play"), in which the child can make adjust ments in their cognitive perceptions and better understand relationships found in their life's ecosystem.

Several different assessment tests are used to monitor the child's progress, and selection depends on the child's presenting problem. Generally, the therapist works individually with the child, although sometimes sessions are structured to include contact time with the parents (e.g., thirty minutes with the child / twenty minutes with the parents), and occasionally parents are requested to engage in parallel therapy processes, such as couple counseling.

Ecosystemic play therapy works particularly well with foster children and adopted children who have spent time in the child welfare system. More than the other models, it captures the life of these children who are often exposed to multiple adult caretakers in a variety of settings. Imagine a child surrounded by foster and adoptive parents, birth parents, the county social worker, the foster family agency social worker, a therapist, a medical doctor, a lawyer in the children's court system, a CASA worker, a judge, and the list goes on. Children are deeply influenced by the people around them, some of whom may have never laid eyes on the child. Ecosystemic play therapy often has a compelling resonance with such children, perhaps because it so closely approximates the world in which they live.

Post-Adoption Services

Healthcare providers, public and private adoption agencies, and school psychologists offer an enormous range of post-adoption services to foster and adopted children and their families. In addition, child welfare service providers, usually social workers or marriage and family therapists, provide needed post-adoption services. To find services, the Child Welfare Information Gateway offers a "National Foster Care & Adoption Directory Search" function at http://www.childwelfare.gov/mfcad that allows for searches of post-adoption services in your area. Figures 10.1 and 10.2 show, respectively, common reasons why families seek services and times when these services may be particularly beneficial.[35] •

• grief and loss issues	• identity formation
• understanding adoption	• birth relative contact
• trust and attachment issues	• medical concerns
• post-institutionalization issues and behaviors	• racial issues
	• school problems

FIGURE 10.1 Reasons for post-adoption services

- Birthdays of the adopted child, siblings, adoptive parents, or birthparents
- Anniversaries relating to the placement of the child in foster care
- Placement in the adoptive home, or the date of the finalization of the adoption
- Holidays, especially Mother's Day or Father's Day, or other holidays where family gatherings are common
- Entering kindergarten or first grade (due to the need to explain adoption to their peers)
- Puberty or adolescence when the child's awareness of his ability to reproduce raises questions about birth and adoption
- The adoptive mother's subsequent pregnancy or another adoption
- The adopted child becomes a mother or father

FIGURE 10.2 Milestones prompting post-adoption services

Adoptive parents tend to have more wealth and resources than the population at large, and thus are more like to utilize therapeutic services. If you are lucky enough to have a high level of financial security, consider yourself blessed. Having the means to assist a child in need is nothing to be ashamed of, particularly if you are willing to invest in services a child needs be successful. In seeking post-adoption services, a good first step is to contact your local child welfare agency. Ask what ser-

---

* Figures 10.1 and 10.2 are adapted from a post-adoption services report published in 2006 by the Child Welfare Information Gateway and available at http://www.childwelfare.gov/pubs/f_postadoption.cfm. The site is a good place to seek additional information about post-adoption services and assistance available in each state.

vices they offer and what services they recommend to adoptive
families in the community. I also advise finding a local adoption support group that can provide a safe community to vent,
commiserate, and exchange knowledge and ideas. One organization, Families Supporting Adoption, hosts a useful website
(www.familiessupporting adoption) that allows for searches of
support groups in your area. A simple Google search for "adoption support groups" will lead to many others you may contact
by phone for further information.

Summary

Therapy and post-adoptions services are available and effective for families looking for assistance. This chapter addresses
only a small sampling of the types of services available for children with specific needs. Typically, therapy models lean in one
of two directions, either focusing on action-oriented models
of behavioral change, or favoring the exploration of the psychological meaning underlying a child's words and actions. If
you are considering adopting a child with special needs, post-
adoption services may be especially useful. Although adopting a "harder-to-place" child does not mean your life will be
constantly consumed by therapy, it does mean you are likely to
confront behavioral, academic, and relational disruptions that
are best addressed in a therapeutic setting. Finding a therapeutic approach that adheres to your family's values and instincts
is vital. The main reason for hope is the number of quality
services available, many of them covered by federal funding
or available at a low cost. These services can help you lead an
adoptive family life that brings joy and satisfaction to your
home, if you take the important first step of seeking help.

Chapter Eleven
Why We Need More Adoptions

Adopting children, especially hard-to-place adoptable children, comes with its joys and tribulations. It can be daunting to read about the high risk for behavior problems in adoptive children or to discover that therapy or other professional services may be needed to ensure your child undergoes healthy development. There is little doubt you will feel the challenge once the child is placed in your home. But every parent feels tested by his child at some point. We don't decide to be parents because it is easy. It's supposed to be a time of learning and adjustment, that's the very nature of parenting—the joy comes in making a difference in a child's life. Personally, I've experienced that joy many times: when Nathan made the whole family laugh at one of his jokes; when Samantha made the honor roll; when Kellie shined in her drama performance; when Joshua struck out the side in Little League; when Jason asked me to play catch; when Danny cuddled with me and announced, "You're my daddy." It's times like those when you feel proud of and close to your children that make the challenges worth it. It's not a question of whether or not adopting a child will bring challenges. I guarantee it will. The question is: Are you up to it? Do you have what it takes to be an adoptive parent? And, if so, what kind of adoption do you want, and what are you capable of handling?

You have options. I realize I've emphasized the great needs of hard-to-place children who are maybe a little older than you originally anticipated, perhaps of a different race or ethnic background, or diagnosed with a medical concern you hadn't anticipated. You may decide those options are not for you— that given your family's needs and resources the right thing to do is to pursue the dream you originally anticipated of a young, healthy, same-race infant. And that's completely appropriate. In fact it's wonderful. Adopting any child, if it's right for your family and that child, is truly a good thing. Years ago when I interviewed adoptive parents for my dissertation, almost every single adoptive parent said they felt as though God, fate, or divine intervention had played a hand in guiding the child into their life for the best interest of the family. As a Mormon, I truly believe that this is true: families are called to adoption, guided to what is right for themselves and their children.

The magnitude of the need is great. If you are willing to change your preferences to suit the available "supply" of waiting adoptable children, then I urge you to do it. With some 115,000 children on the child welfare rolls currently awaiting adoption,1 it is difficult to overstate the potential social benefit couples can affect by choosing to adopt children who have been traditionally ignored in the system. By reorienting your notion of what adoption may mean to your family, whether this implies adopting a child of a different race or ethnicity, of an older age, or with special medical needs or a troubled family history, you can make a tremendous difference. With such adoptions the trials you face may be especially difficult, but there are plenty of clinical and therapeutic services that are available to help.

Remember we need more adoptions in America. As a society, there are numerous social benefits to the cultivation of a pro-adoption culture. Children who remain without a permanent home are more likely to commit crimes, more likely to have mental health concerns, and perhaps most importantly, assuming these children continue to live without a healthy model for family interaction, more likely to perpetuate family dysfunction in their own children. Adoption under the guidance of stable and consistent caregivers is one of the best means to break this cycle.

There are several ways to find the right kind of adoption for you. As a rule, I encourage prospective adoptive couples to attend orientation meetings from multiple types of adoption agencies before committing. Common practice for many adoption agencies, legally required in some states, is that you commit to adopt through one agency at a time. That means you need to be sure you've picked the right one. Determining what method of adoption you prefer—public or child welfare agency adoption, private agency adoption, international adoption, and so on—will suggest where to begin. From there I recommend visiting several agencies, including one or two that specialize in an unconventional method of adoption. Generally, the more educated you can be about adoption practices and policies, the better continuity you will find between what you hope for and expect and your eventual adoption experience.

A simple Google search will yield good resources for local listings in your area, and you can find additional resources in the appendix of this book. Most states have a Child Protective Services (CPS) agency on either a state or county level. They go by different names and have their own organizational protocols. In California, child protective services is called the Department of Children and Family Services (DCFS) and is administered on a county basis. In Illinois it is also called DCFS, but it is operated on the statewide level. When seeking information your state or county's CPS agency is a good place to start. You can also look for private adoption agencies in your area. Many private adoption agencies are linked with religious organizations, some of which require prospective adoptive couples to claim specific religious affiliations. Others do not have such mandates, so make sure to ask questions about the organization's requirements and fellowship when you call to make inquiries. Most private agencies specialize in particular areas such as open adoptions or international adoptions, and it is wise to find an agency that has a good reputation and experience administering the type of adoption you wish to pursue.

Local professionals who specialize in facilitating adoptions (i.e., lawyers or medical doctors) will often advertise locally. In choosing independent providers, the basic economic rule applies: caveat emptor—let the buyer beware. Most providers are trustworthy, honest, and professional in their dealings with prospective adoptive couples but unfortunately some are not and each candidate's qualifications and background should be individually scrutinized. Adoption attorneys should be able to give you an up-front estimate of their service fees. If they can't, find someone else. Most will stipulate that if unforeseen issues arise their costs are subject to change, and this should not be cause for concern (remember lawyers generally bill at an hourly rate, not a flat fee).* Often word of mouth referrals from people whom you know and trust, those who've had good experiences working with these professionals, are the best form of evaluation.

Regardless of what type of adoption you select and what agency you choose, you will have to do the standard finger-

---

* For instance, if the child's birth parent claims the child is Native American, under the Indian Child Welfare Act the appropriate tribe must be contacted to verify whether the child is officially part of the tribe and to determine jurisdiction. Another example would be if one of the birth parents is in the military. Under the Soldiers and Sailors Civil Relief Act, court proceedings regarding a military person's child custody follow unique guidelines. Cases such as these can cause legal fees to rise. Competent independent adoption lawyers should understand these guidelines in advance and be able to predict the associated costs. If they cannot, they probably lack the experience to handle your case.

printing and background checks. You'll go through several hours of parent training specific to adoption and foster care. You'll do a home study that will include interviews of you, your spouse, and any children or other relatives living in the home. Generally, the agency will do a home inspection and provide you with a list of items you will need to change to prepare your home for a child. The list is often very particular. Swimming pools, ponds, or other water sources may need to be covered or secured with protective fencing. Locks may be required for medicines, kitchen knives, and weapons; you may need to install a fire extinguisher or smoke alarm; secured gates to protect a child from fireplaces and stairs. Usually the social workers will do a preliminary walk-through of your home, noting changes they expect, and then return once you've updated the house and are ready for a final inspection. In the event you move homes in the middle of the process, you'll need to have the agency redo the home inspection to relicense your new home. It is important to realize that if you go through all of these processes with an agency and choose to switch to a different agency, you'll most likely have to start over from the beginning. This is why it is so important to be absolutely sure an agency is right for you before making a commitment. Far too many couples invest time, energy, and funds into the background check and home study, only to realize they are dissatisfied with the agency they've chosen.

I've tried to write this book in the style of a conversation with you about adoption because I believe what most prospective parents are looking for is reliable information, not academese. Frequently, my wife and I have had people in our social network mention they are interested in adopting. We invite them over for dinner and, after eating, sprawl out on the living room couches to continue the conversation while the kids go play. In a way, this book represents an extension of that conversation. By no means does it tell you everything you will need to know in the months and years after you've adopted. Instead, I've chosen to emphasize what I hope are the things you need right now to choose an adoption experience that is right for you.

Remember that a "one-size-fits-all" approach to adoption doesn't capture the complexity and diversity of contemporary adoptive families in America, nor will such an approach be useful in your adoptive search. With so many different kinds of adoptive family structures, patterns, and practices by which to model your experience, it is a good idea to begin by focusing your search. Pre-adoption planning should always include a frank, realistic discussion about your family's goals and limitations in raising the child. From there you can generate a list of relevant agencies and organizations and begin to evaluate how well they align with your specific preferences and needs. This process may take some time but it is time in which you will be learning more about what it means to adopt and what your family will need to do in order to prepare.

Let me conclude this book the way it began—with a personal story about my adoptive experience. To me this moment captures the essence of what it means to adopt exceptional children. When our daughter Samantha's and our son Jason's adoptions were finalized, our family was still living in Springfield, Illinois. In the Mormon faith, adopted children enjoy a special religious ceremony called a temple sealing, which consecrates the family relationship. We chose to have this done in the Nauvoo, Illinois, temple, a holy site with historic roots to the earlier adherents of our faith. Although the temple was only two hours away, we made a weekend trip out of it, staying across the Mississippi River, in Iowa, the night before. On the way to the temple, as we drove over the gently rolling prairie spreading out from the river, I noticed the radiance that bejewels the Midwest in late fall. The trees were ablaze with hues of red, yellow, and orange, and I thought of how the colors symbolized the diversity of the adoption experience. In the past, we had relished the experience of adopting infants, but this day was about two older children joining our eternal family, children we knew to be more behaviorally difficult but in need of a home. All five of our children were with us as we drove up to the temple, located atop a hill overlooking the great river. The day was clear. I could hardly contain my joy as we entered the temple and prepared for the ceremony. The children and guests entered the holy room first, waiting for my wife and me to join them. The minister officiating the ceremony, called a "sealer," counseled us. He said that in the eyes of God it were as if these children were born to us, and on hearing his blessing, I thought—not for the first time—of the immensity of the adoptive experience.

Born to birth parents with an uncertain history, Samantha and Jason face a number of cognitive, emotional, and behavioral difficulties. Challenges such as these do not instantly vanish with adoption. But the loving bond we feel toward them is no different than if had they been born to us. As we knelt around the altar that brisk autumn day, holding hands and united as a family, I knew that adoption was and would always be one of the greatest blessings of my life. Though our family has experienced many different kinds of adoptions and learned much through the milestones of our journey, one resonating truth rings out—that the kinds of adoptions we chose were right for our family. I hope this book will help you make the type of adoption choice that is right for yours.

Appendix: Agency Listings, Treatment Information, Legal and Financial Resources

Agencies
These resources are not intended as an exhaustive list, but a place to start with the largest, most reputable agencies on a national level.

Public and Child Welfare Adoptions
National Foster Care & Adoption Directory Search
   http://wwwhttp://www.childwelfare.gov/nfcad/
Adopting Children Through a Public Agency (Foster Care)
   http://www.childwelfare.gov/adoption/adoptive/foster_care.cfm
Children in Foster Care Awaiting Adoption
   http://www.adoptuskids.org

Private/Religious Adoptions
Association of Jewish Family & Children's Agencies
5750 Park Heights Avenue, Baltimore, MD 21215
Phone: (800) 634-7346
http://www.ajfca.org/

Bethany Christian Services
901 Eastern Ave, NE
PO Box 294, Grand Rapids, MI 49501-0294
Phone: (616) 224-7610, (800) 238-4269
http://www.bethany.org/

Catholic Charities

Sixty-Six Canal Center Plaza, Suite 600, Alexandria, VA 22314

Phone: (703) 549-1390

http://www.catholiccharitiesusa.org/netcommunity/adoptionwebsite

LDS Family Services

132 South State St., #100, Salt Lake City, UT 84111-1506

Phone: (800) 537-2229 or (801) 240-6500

http://www.itsaboutlove.org

International Adoptions

U.S. State Department Intercountry Adoption website

U.S. Department of State, Office of Children's Issues, SA-29

2201 C Street, NW, Washington, DC 20520

Phone: (888) 407-4747 (U.S. or Canada)

(202) 501-4444 (other locations)

http://www.adoption.state.gov/

The Alliance for Children

464 Hillside Ave., Suite 300, Needham, MA 02494

Phone: (781) 444-7148

http://www.allforchildren.org/

Holt International

P.O. Box 2880, 1195 City View, Eugene, OR 97402

Phone: (541) 687-2202

http://www.holtinternational.org/

Christian World Adoption

777 South Allen Road, Flat Rock, NC 28731

Phone: (828) 693-7007, (888) 972-3678

http://www.cwa.org/

Adopt International & Domestic Services

1000 Brannan, Suite 301, San Francisco, CA 94103

Phone: (415) 934-0300

http://www.adoptinter.org/

Books
Available on the Web
AdoptionBooks.com

    http://www.adoptionbooks.com

ComeUnity

    http://www.comeunity.com/adoption/books/index.html

Tapestry Books

    http://www.tapestrybooks.com

NTI Upstream

    http://www.nitupstream.com

For Adoptive Parents
Brodzinsky, David M., Schechter, Marshall D., & Henig, Robin M. *Being Adopted: The Lifelong Search for Self.* New York: Doubleday, 1992.

Eldridge, Sherrie. *20 Things Adoptive Parents Need to Succeed.* New York: Delta, 2009.

Keck, Gregory C. & Kupecky, Regina. Adopting the Hurt Child: *Hope for Families with Special-Needs Kids.* Colorado Springs: Nav Press, 2009.

Watkins, Mary & Fisher, Susan. *Talking with Young Children About Adoption.* New Haven: Yale University Press, 2009.

Weir, Kyle. *Coming Out of the Adoptive Closet.* Lanham, MD: University Press of America, 2003.

For Younger Children
Curtis, Jamie Lee. *Tell Me Again About the Night I was Born.* New York: Harper Collins, 2000.

Kasza, Keiko. *A Mother for Choco*. New York: Penguin Group, 1996.

Rosove, Lori. *Rosie's Family: An Adoption Story*. Oakland: Asia Press, 2001.

Bergen, Lisa Tawn. *God Found Us You*. New York: Harper Collins, 2000.

For Older Children and Adolescents

Crook, Marion. *The Face in the Mirror: Teenagers and Adoption*. Vancouver, CA: Arsenal Pulp Press, 2000.

Gorbett, Danea. *Adopted Teens Only: A Survival Guide to Adolescence*. Bloomington: iUniverse Star, 2007.

Slade, Suzanne Buckingham. *Adopted: The Ultimate Teen Guide*. Lanham, MD: The Scarecrow Press, 2009.

Riley, Debbie with Meeks, John. *Beneath the Mask: Understanding Adopted Teens*, Washington, DC: CASE, 2009.

Ballard, Robert L. *Pieces of Me: Who Do I Want to Be?* Warren, NJ: EMK Press, 2009.

Lowell, Pamela. *Returnable Girl*. Oregon City: Marshall Cavendish Children's Books, 2006.

Eldridge, Sherrie. *Twenty Things Adopted Kids Wish Their Adoptive Parents Knew*. New York: Delta, 1999.

Magazines

Adoptive Families
    http://www.adoptivefamilies.com/
Adoption Month E-Magazine
    http://e-magazine.adoption.com/
Adoption Today
    http://www.adoptinfo.net/
Fostering Families Today
    http://www.fosteringfamiliestoday.com/
Rainbow Kids
    http://www.rainbowkids.com/

Websites
The Adoption Guide
> http://www.theadoptionguide.com/

Adoption.com
> http://www.adoption.com

AdoptUsKids.org
> http://www.adoptuskids.org/

Adoption.org
> http://www.adoption.org

Adoption/Fostercare About.com
> http://adoption.about.com/

Child Welfare Information Gateway
> http://www.childwelfare.gov

Dave Thomas Foundation for Adoption
> http://www.davethomasfoundation.org

Evan B. Donaldson Adoption Institute
> http://www.adoptioninstitute.org/

North American Council on Adoptable Children
> http://www.nacac.org/

Treatment Information
Child Welfare Information Gateway
> http://www.childwelfare.gov/pubs/f_therapist.cfm

American Association for Marriage and Family Therapy
> http://www.aamft.org

The Theraplay Institute
> http://www.theraplay.org

Adopting.org
> http://www.adopting.org/adoptions/adoption-counseling-counselors-therapists.html

American Counseling Association
> http:www.counseling.org/Resources

Legal Guidance
The National Center for Adoption Law & Policy (NCALP)
Capital University Law School
303 E. Broad Street
Columbus, Ohio 43215
Phone: (614) 236-6730
http://www.law.capital.edu/adoption/

National Adoption Foundation (for financial support, grants, & legal referrals)
36 Mill Plain Road
Danbury, CT 06811
http://www.nafadopt.org/
e-mail: nafadopt@aol.com

Avvo.com (for free legal advice on adoption)
http://www.avvo.com/free-legal-advice/adoption

Adoption & Child Welfare Law Site
 http://www.adoptionchildwelfarelaw.org/adoption_pros.php

Financial Support
Adoption Assistance Program (AAP)
 http://www.childwelfare.gov/adoption/adopt_assistance/

North American Council on Adoptable Children
(for adoption subsidy information)
http://www.nacac.org/adoptionsubsidy/adoptionsubsidy.html

Visit Our Website
For more information about adoption, the author, or the book *The Choice of a Lifetime: What You Need to Know Before Adopting,* please visit our website at www.thechoiceofalifetime.net.

Notes

Chapter One: Social and Legal Changes Affecting Adoption

1. McGoldrick, M. & Walsh, F., "Death and the Family Life Cycle," in *The Expanded Family Life Cycle: Individual, Family, and Social Perspectives,* ed. Carter, B., & McGoldrick, M. (Boston: Allyn & Bacon, 2005).

2. Bartlett, C., "Transracial Adoption: A Triumph of Love over Race?" *Family Therapy Magazine,* May-June 2004,16-21; Schwartz, L., "Families by Choice: Adoptive and Foster Families," in *Handbook of Family Development and Intervention,* ed. Nichols, W., Pace-Nichols, M., Becvar, D., and Napier, A. (New York: John Wiley & Sons, 2000).

3. U.S. Department of Health and Human Services, Administration for Children and Families, *Perspectives of Families and Staff Supported by the Adoption Opportunities Program: A Report to Congress on Barriers and Success Factors in Adoptions from Foster Care* (Washington, DC: U.S. Government Printing Office, 2007).

4. See note 2.

5. Weir, K , *Coming Out of the Adoptive Closet* (Lanham, MA.

University Press of America, 2003). One other important factor may come into play, and that is the notion of divine will or destiny some adoptive parents feel is inherent in the process of adopting their child. As I've shown previously, seeking the guidance of God or a "higher power" may be instrumental in your decision-making about adoption.

6. Weir, K., "The Many Faces of Adoption," *Family Therapy Magazine,* May/June 2004, 8-13.

7. *Adoption and Safe Families Act of 1997,* Public Law 105-89, 105th Congress, *U.S. Statutes at Large,* 111 (1997): 2115

8. U.S. Department of Health and Human Services, Administration for Children and Families, Children's Bureau, "AF-CARS Report #17: Preliminary Estimates for FY 2009," http://www.acf.hhs.gov/programs/cb/stats_research/afcars/tar/report10.htm (accessed October 25, 2010).

9. Kernan, E., & Lansford, J., "Providing for the Best Interests of the Child?" The Adoption and Safe Families Act of 1997," *Journal of Applied Developmental Psychology,* 25, no. 5 (2004): 523-39.

Chapter Two: Adoption Methods and the Myth of Disruption

1. U.S. Department of Health and Human Services, Administration for Children and Families, National Adoption Information Clearinghouse, "Adoption: Numbers and Trends," 2004, http://naic.acf.hss.gov. (accessed March 20, 2004).

2. Barth, R. & Berry, M., *Adoption and Disruption: Rates, Risks, and*

Responses (Hawthorne, NY: Adline de Gruyter, 1988); Cowan, A., "New Strategies to Promote the Adoption of Older Children out of Foster Care," *Children & Youth Services Review, 26,* no. 11 (2004): 1007-1020; Rosenthal, J.A., "Outcomes of Adoption of Children with Special Needs," *The Future of Children,* 3, no. 1 (1993): 77-88; Whiteman, V.E., "A Needs Assessment toward Developing a Model Training Program for Adoptive Parents of an Older Child," *Dissertation Abstracts International,* 64 no. 2-A (2003): 401.

3. Groze, V., "Special Needs Adoption," *Child and Youth Services Review,* 8 (1986): 363-73. See note 2.

4. Wrobel, G., Hendrickson, Z. & Grotevant, H., "Adoption" in *Children's Needs III: Development, Prevention, and Intervention,* ed., Bear, G. & Minke, K. (Washington, DC: National Association of School Psychologists, 2006), 675-88.

5. Harper-Dorton, K., "Post-Legal Adoption Treatment Groups: Intervening with Families Who Experience Failed Adoption," in *Crossing Boundaries and Developing Alliances through Group Work,* ed., Lindsay, J., Turcotte, D., & Hopmeyer, E. (New York: Hawthorne Press, 2003), 193-208.

6. U.S. Department of Commerce, Bureau of the Census. *Adopted Children and Stepchildren, 2000* (Washington, DC: U.S. Government Printing Office, 2003), 15.

7. U.S. Department of Health and Human Services, Administration for Children and Families, National Adoption Information Clearinghouse, "State Regulation of Adoption Expenses," 2005, http:www.adoptionamerica.com/stateregulations.htm (accessed May 26, 2009). The word "approximately" denotes the fact that statutes are constantly being revised and updated. The information in this citation is current through January 2005.

8. Ibid.

9. Chasnoff, I., Schwartz L., Pratt, C., Neuberger, G., *Risk and Promise: A Handbook for Parents Adopting a Child from Overseas* (Chicago: NTI Upstream, 2006).

10. Spar, K., *Foster Care and Adoption Statistics*, report prepared for the House Subcommittee on Human Resources, 1997, http://www.casa.net/library/foster-care/fost.htm (accessed May 28, 2009).

11. See note 6.

12. *Child Citizenship Act of 2000.* Public Law, 106-395, 106th Congress, *U.S. Statutes at Large* 114 (2000): 1631.

13. The Hague Conference on Private International Law. *Convention of 29 May 1993 on Protection of Children and Co-operation in Respect of Intercountry Adoption*, entry into force: 1-V-1995, http:www.hcch.net/index_en.php?act=conventions.text&cid=69 (accessed October 25, 2010).

14. Schwartz, L. "Families by Choice: Adoptive and Foster Families," in *Handbook of Family Development and Intervention*, ed., Nichols, W.C., Pace-Nichols, M., Becvar, D., & Napier, A. (New York: John Wiley & Sons, 2000), 259.

15. See note 15, p.15.

16. Ibid.

17. Ibid.

18. Boyd, F., *Black Families in Therapy* (New York: Guilford Press, 1989).

Chapter Three: Diversity Within Contemporary Adoptive Families

1. Weir, K. *Coming Out of the Adoptive Closet* (Lanham, MD: University Press of America, 2003).

2. Stolley, K., "Statistics on Adoption in the United States," *The Future of Children: Adoption*, 3, no.1 (1993): 26-42; U.S. Department of Commerce, Bureau of the Census. *Adopted Children and Stepchildren, 2000.* (Washington, DC: U.S. Government Printing Office, 2003).

3. See note 2, U.S. Department of Commerce, Bureau of the Census, 2003.

4. Bartlet, C., "Transracial Adoption: A Triumph of Love over Race," *Family Therapy Magazine*, May-June, 2004, 16-21; McRoy, R., "Achieving Same-Race Adoptive Placements for African American Children: Culturally Sensitive Practice Approaches," *Child Welfare*, 76, no. 1 (1997): 85-104; Schwartz, L., "Families by Choice: Adoptive and Foster Families," in *Handbook of Family Development and Intervention*, ed., Nichols, W.C., Pace-Nichols, M., Becvar, D., & Napier, A. (New York: John Wiley & Sons, 2000), 259.

5. Gyllenhall, N., *Losing Isaiah*, (Hollywood, CA: Paramount Pictures, 1995).

6. Rodriguez, V. & Xocop, D., "Making Friends: Jairo Eli Xocop of Comalapa, Guatemala," *Friend*, January, 2005.

7. Weir, K. & Becker, K., "Adoption Family Rituals: Celebrating Tradition, Connection, and Contact" (article presented to the Association of Counselor Educators and Supervisors Conference in Park City, Utah, October, 2002).

8. U.S. Department of Commerce, Bureau of the Census. *Adopted Children and Stepchildren, 2000* (Washington, DC: U.S. Government Printing Office, 2003); Weir, K., "The Many Faces of Adoption," *Family Therapy Magazine*, May/June 2004, 8-13.

9. Evan B. Donaldson Institute, "Foster Care Fact Sheet," http://:www.adoptioninstitute.org/FactOverview/foster.html (accessed May 26, 2009).

10. Weir, K., "The Many Faces of Adoption." *Family Therapy Magazine*, May/June 2004, 8-13. See note 2.

11.Kirk, H., *Shared Fate: A Theory and Method of Adoptive Relationships* (Port Angeles:, WA: Ben-Simon, 1984).

Chapter Four: How Well Do Adopted Children Fare?

1. Associated Press, "Boy Sent Back to Russia; Adoption Ban Urged," MSNBC, April 9, 2010.

2. Kirrschner, D., "Adoption Psychopathology and the Adopted Child Syndrome," *Directions in Child and Adolescent Therapy*, 2, no 6. (1995); Kirschner, D. *Adoption: Unchartered Waters* (Woodbury, NY: Juneau Press, 2006).

3. Verrier, N., *The Primal Wound: Understanding the Adopted Child* (Lafayette, CA: Nancy Verrier, self-published, 1993).

4. Gorman, P., "Resisting the Deficit View of Adoption," *Family Therapy Magazine*, May/June 2004, 22-25.

5. Ibid.

6. Benson, P., Sharma, A., & Roehlkepartain, E., *Growing Up Adopted* (Minneapolis: Search Institute, 2004); Kadushin, A. & Reitz, M., *Child Welfare Services* (New York: MacMillan, 1988); Nickman, S., et al., "Children in Adoptive Families: Overview and Update," *Journal of the American Academy of Child and Adolescent Psychiatry*, 44, no. 10 (2005): 987-996.

7. Miller, B., Fan, X., Christensen, M., Grotevant, H., & van Dulmen, M., "Comparisons of Adopted and Nonadopted Adolescents in a Large, Nationally Representative Sample, *Child Development*, 71 (2000): 1458-1473.

8. Weir, K., "How Well Do Adopted Kids Fare?" (workshop presented for the American Association for Marriage and Family Therapy Conference, recorded and published by Blue Sky Broadcast, Austin, TX, October 21, 2006); see note 7.

9. Carter, B. "Becoming Parent," in *The Expanded Family Life Cycle: Individual, Family, and Social Perspectives, 3rd ed.,* ed., Carter, B., & McGoldrick, M. (Boston: Allyn and Bacon, 2005); Miller, R., "Do Children Make a Marriage Unhappy?" *Marriage and Families*, 5 (2001): 13-18. See notes 4,6.

10. See note 9, Carter, 2005.

11. See note 4; note 6, Benson, Sharma, & Roelkepartain, 2004.

12. See note 6, Benson, Sharma, & Roehlkepartain, 2004; Kadushin & Reitz, 1988.

13. Rosenthal, J., "Outcomes of Adoption of Children with Special Needs," *The Future of Children*, 3, no. 1 (1993) 77-88.

14. Bimmel, N., et al., "Problem Behavior of Internationally Adopted Adolescents: A Review and Meta-Analysis," *Harvard*

Review of Psychiatry, 11, (2003): 64-77; Jaffari-Bimmel, N., "Development and Adjustment of Adopted Adolescents. Longitudinal and Concurrent Factors" (PhD diss., Leiden University, 2005).

15. See note 14, Bimmel, 2003.

16. Nickman, S., et al., "Children in Adoptive Families: Overview and Update," *Journal of the American Academy of Child and Adolescent Psychiatry*, 44 no. 10 (2005) 987-996.

17. Ibid.

Chapter Five: Age of Placement, Placement History, and Attachment

1. Benson, P., Sharma, A., & Roehlkepartain, E., *Growing Up Adopted* (Minneapolis: Search Institute, 1994); Kadushin, A. & Reitz, M., *Child Welfare Services* (New York: MacMillan, 1988).

2. Barth, R. & Berry, M., *Adoption and Disruption: Rates, Risks, and Responses* (Hawthorne, NY: Adline de Gruyter, 1988); Berry, M. & Barth, R., "Behavior Problems of Children Adopted When Older," *Children & Youth Services Review*, 11 (1989): 221-238.

3. See note 2, Berry, M. & Barth, R., 1989.

4. Foster Care Support Foundation, "Transition Guidelines," from *Parent Life* "5 Steps to Transition," 2009 http://www.fostercares.org/Default.aspx?tabid=83 (accessed October 28, 2010).

5. Broderick, C., *Marriage and the Family*, 4ᵗʰ ed. (Englewood Cliffs, NJ: Prentice Hall, 1992); Weir, K., "The Magnifying Effect: The Recursive Benefits of Marriage and Adoption Throughout the Adoptive Family Life-Cycle," *Journal of Law & Family Studies*, 6, no. 1 (2004); Weir, K., "Repairing Adoptive and Foster Attachments," *Family Therapy Magazine*, 5, no. 5 (Sept./Oct. 2006), 17-20.

6. Bowlby, J., "Mother-child Separation," in *Mental Health and Infant Development*, ed., Soddy, K. (Oxford: Basic Books, 1956).

7. See note 4, Weir, 2006.

8. Hallas, D., "The Attachment Relationship Between Foster Care Parents and Foster Children," *Dissertation Abstracts International*, 60, no. 11-B (2000): 5432; Maxey, D., "The Relationship of Parental Gender, Number of Placements, and Length of Time in an Orphanage on the Perceptions of Parents Scoring the Attachment Disordered Behaviors of their Foster or Adoptive Child," *Dissertation Abstracts International*, 65 no. 2-B, (2004): 1063; Schofield, G. & Beek, M., "Providing a Secure Base: Parenting Children in Long-term Foster Family Care," *Attachment and Human Development*, 7 no. 1 (2005): 3-25.

9. Perry, W., Pollard, R., Blakley, T., et al., "Childhood Trauma, the Neurobiology of Adaptation and Use-Dependent Development of the Brain: How States Become Traits," *Infant Mental Health Journal*, 16 (1995): 271-79; Glaser, D., "Child Abuse and Neglect and the Brain—A Review," *Journal of Child Psychology and Psychiatry*, 41(2000): 97-116.

10. See note 8, Hallas, 2000; Maxey, 2004; Schofield & Beck, 2005.

11. See note 4, Weir, 2006.

12. Gissler, K., "How to Hug a Rock" (master's thesis, University of Illinois at Springfield, n.d.)

13. Erikson, E., *Childhood and Society* (New York: W.W. Norton & Company, 1950)

14. Bowlby, J., *Attachment and Loss,* vols. 1-3 (London: Hogarth Press; New York, Basic Books; Harmondsworth, UK: Penguin, 1969-1982).

15. Ainsworth, P., Blehar, M., Waters, E., & Wall, S., *Patterns of Attachment* (Hillsdale, NJ: Erlbaum: 1978).

16. Jernberg A. & Booth P., *Theraplay: Helping Parents and Children Build Better Relationships through Attachment-Based Play,* 2nd ed. (San Francisco: Jossey-Bass, 1999).

17. See note 14.

18. Hughes, D., *Attachment-Focused Family Therapy* (New York: W.W. Norton & Company, 2007); Hughes, D. *Facilitating Developmental Attachment: The Road to Emotional Recovery and Behavioral Change in Foster and Adopted Children* (Northvale, NJ: Jason Aronson, 1997).

19. See note 18, Hughes, D., 2007.

20. Ibid.

21. Ibid., 130.

22. American Psychiatric Association, *Diagnostic and Statistical Manual of Mental Disorders,* rev. 4th ed., Washington, DC, 2000.

23. Ibid.

24. Ibid.

Chapter Six: Medical Special Needs Children

1. Boyse, K., Boujaoude, L., & Laundy, J., "Children with Chronic Conditions," University of Michigan Health Systems report, http://www.med.umich.edu/1lbr/yourchild/chronic.htm (accessed May 8, 2008).

2. Byrd, A., "Gender Complementarity and Child-rearing: Where Tradition and Science Agree" (paper presented at the Adoption and Family Systems Conference, Brigham Young University, Provo, UT, September 26, 2003).

3. Renwick, A., "Medical Issues in Adoption," KidsHealth, The Newmours Foundation, September 2008 http://kidshealth.org/parent/positive/family/medical_adopt.html (accessed October 28, 2010).

4. Ibid.

5. *Adoption and Safe Families Act of 1997,* Public Law 105-89, 105th Congress, *U.S. Statutes at Large,* 111 (1997): 2115

6. Child Welfare Information Gateway, "Adoption Assistance for Children Adopted From Foster Care," (Washington, DC: U.S. Department of Health and Human Services, June 2004), http://www.childwelfare.gov/pubs/sp_subsid.cfm (accessed October 28, 2010).

7. Ibid.

8. Ibid.

9. Kirk, H., *Shared Fate: A Theory and Method of Adoptive Relationships* (Port Angeles:, WA: Ben-Simon, 1984).

Chapter Seven: Parental and Prenatal Care History

1. Child Welfare Information Gateway, "Definitions of Child Abuse and Neglect: Summary of State Laws," (Washington, DC: U.S. Department of Health and Human Services, July 2009), http://www.childwelfare.gov/systemwide/laws_policies/statutes/define.cfm (accessed October 29, 2010).

2. Child Welfare Information Gateway, "What is Child Abuse and Neglect?" (Washington, DC: U.S. Department of Health and Human Services, April 2009), http://www.childwelfare.gov/pubs/factsheets/whatiscan.pdf (accessed October 29, 2010).

3. *The Child Abuse Prevention and Treatment Act*, U.S. Code 42 (1996), § 5106g.

4. Evans, P., The Verbal Abuse Site, http://www.verbalabuse.com (accessed September 26, 2009).

5. Garbarino, J. & Garbariino A., *Emotional Maltreatment of Children*, 2nd ed., (Chicago: National Committee to Prevent Child Abuse, 1994); American Humane Association, "What is Emotional Abuse?" http://www.americanhumane.org/about-us/newsroom/fact-sheets/emotional-abuse.html (accessed October 29, 2010).

6. See note 2.

7. See note 3.

8. National Center on Addiction and Substance Abuse at Columbia University (CASA), *Family Matters: Substance Abuse and the American Family* (New York: CASA, 2005).

9. Ibid.

10. *Whitner v. South Carolina*, 492 S.E. 2d 777 (S.C. 1997).

11. National Advocates for Pregnant Women, "Whitner v. South Carolina Fact Sheet," http://www.advocatesforpregnantwomen.org/facts/whitner.htm (accessed October 29, 2010); Drug Policy Alliance, "Whitner v. the State of South Carolina," June 2004 (accessed October 29, 2010); *McKnight v. South Carolina*, 576 S.E. 2d 168 (S.C. 2001).

12. Chasnoff, I., *The Nature of Nurture: Biology, Environment, and the Drug-Exposed Child* (Chicago: NTI Upstream, 2001), 2.

13. See note 8.

14. Santrock, J., *Life-Span Development*, 12th ed. (New York: McGraw-Hill, 2009).

15. Coles, C. et al., "Effects of Prenatal Alcohol Exposure at School Age: I. Physical and Cognitive Development," *Neurotoxicology and Teratology*, 13 (1991): 357-67; Astley S., Olson H., & Kerns K. et al., "Neuropsychological and Behavioral Outcomes from a Comprehensive Magnetic Resonance Study of Children with Fetal Alcohol Spectrum Disorders," *Canadian Journal of Clinical Pharmacology*," 16(2009):e178-e201.

16. See note 14.

17. Weng X., Odouli R., & Li D-K., "Maternal Caffeine Consumption During Pregnancy and the Risk of Miscarriage: A Prospective Cohort Study," *American Journal of Obstetrical Gynecology*, 198, no. 279 (2008): e1-279.e8.

18. Li Y., Gilliland F., & Berhane K., "Effects of In Utero and Tobacco Smoke Exposure on Lung Function in Boys and Girls With and Without Asthma," *American Journal of Respiratory and Critical Care Medicine*," 162 (2000): 2097-2104; U.S. Department of Health and Human Services, *The Health Consequences of Involuntary Exposure to Tobacco Smoke: A Report of the Surgeon General* (Atlanta, GA: U.S. Department of Health and Human Services, Centers for Disease Control and Prevention, Coordinating Center for Health Promotion, National Center for Chronic Disease Prevention and Health Promotion, Office of Smoking and Health, 2006).

19. Chasnoff, I., *The Mystery of Risk: Drugs, Alcohol, Pregnancy, and the Vulnerable Child* (Chicago: NTI Upstream, 2010).

20. Wouldes et al., "Maternal Methamphetamine Use During Pregnancy and Child Outcome: What Do We Know?" *New Zealand Medical Journal*, 117, no. 1206 (2004).

21. Wilkie, S. "Global Overview of Drinking Recommendations and Guidelines," *Alcohol In Moderation Digest,* supp. 2, no. 4 (1997): 4; du Florey, D., et al., "A European Concerted Action: Maternal Alcohol Consumption and its Relation to the Outcome of Pregnancy and Development at 18 Months," *International Journal of Epidemiology*, supp. 1, no. 21 (1992).

22. See note 14.

23. Ibid.

24. About.com, http://pediatrics.about.com/od/childabuse/a/05_abuse_stats.htm (accessed July 21, 2010).

25. Streisguth, A., "Offspring Effects of Prenatal Alcohol Exposure from birth to 25 Year: The Seattle Prospective Longitudinal Study," *Journal of Clinical Psychology in Medical Settings*, 14 (2007): 81-101.

26. U.S. Department of Health and Human Services, Administration for Children and Families, *Child Maltreatment*, 2007, (Washington, DC: U.S. Government Printing Office, 2005).

27. Ibid.

28. Perry, B., Pollard R., Blakey T., et al., "The Neuroarcheology of Childhood Maltreatment: The Neurodevelopmental Costs of Adverse Childhood Events" in *The Cost of Maltreatment: Who Pays? We All Do*, ed., Franey K., Geffner R., & Falconer R. (San Diego, CA: Family Violence and Sexual Assault Institute, 2009), 15-29; Oates, R., *The Spectrum of Abuse: Assessment, Treatment, and Prevention*, 1st ed. (London: Routledge, 1996).

29. See note 28, Oates, R., 1996.

Chapter Eight: Demographic Variables and Life Chances

1. Bean R., Perry, B., & Bedell, T., "Developing Culturally Competent Marriage and Family Therapists: treatment Guidelines for Non-African-American Therapists Working with African-American Families," *Journal of Marital and Family Therapy*, 28, no. 2 (2002): 153-64.

2. U.S. Department of Health and Human Services, Office of Minority Health, "What is Cultural Competency?" 2009, http://www.omhrc.gov/templates/browse.aspx?lvl=2&lvlID=11 (accessed Oct. 29, 2010).

3. See the National Center for Cultural Competence website for a comprehensive portal to both scholarly and governmental work on cultural competence, http://www11.gerogetown.edu/research/gucchd/nccc/ (accessed, July 15, 2010).

4. Vonk, E., "Cultural Competence for Transracial Adoptive Parents," *Social Work*, 46, no.3 (2001): 246-55.

5. Silverman, A., "Outcomes of Transracial Adoption," *The Future of Children*, 3, no. 1 (1993): 104-18.

6. Sharma, A., McGue, M., & Bensen P., "The Emotional and Behavioral Adjustment of United States Adopted Adolescents: Part 1. An Overview," *Children & Youth Services Review*, 18 (1996): 83-100.

7. Gill, O. & Jackson, B., *Adoption and Race: Black, Asian, and Mixed Race Children in White Families* (London: Palgrave Macmillan, 1983).

8. National Association of Black Social Workers, "Preserving Families of African Ancestry," 2003 http://www.nabsw.org/mserver/PreservingFamilies.aspx (accessed November 2, 2009).

9. Glenn, N., "Values, Attitudes, and the State of American Marriage," in *Promises to Keep: Decline and Renewal of Marriage in America*, ed., Blakenhorn, D. & Elshtain J. (Lanham, MD: Rowman and Littlefield, 1996), 15-33; Glenn, N., "A Cri-

tique of Twenty Family and Marriage and Family Textbooks," *Family Relations*, 46, no.3 (2006): 197-208.

10. See note 4.

11. Randolph, T. & Holtzman, M. "The Role of Heritage Camps in Identity Development among Korean Transnational Adoptees: A Relational Dialectics Approach," *Adoption Quarterly*, 13, no. 2 (2010): 75-99.

12. Lancaster, C. & Nelson, K., "Where Attachment Meets Acculturation: Three Cases of International Adoption," *The Family Journal: Counseling and Therapy for Couples and Families*, 17, no.4 (2009): 302-11.

13. Adamec, C. & Pierce W., *The Encyclopedia of Adoption* (New York: Facts on File, 1991).

14. Associated Press, "New Romanian Adoption Law Takes Effect," AP Online, January 1, 2005, http://www.highbeam.com/doc/1P1-103889530.html (accessed November 1, 2010).

15. The U.S. Department of Health and Human Services, Administration for Children and Families, "Adoption and Foster Care Analysis and Reporting System," 2009, http://www.acf.hhs.gov/programs/cb/stats_research/afcars/tar/report10.htm (accessed November 1, 2010).

Chapter Nine: Human Development and Adoption

1. Kalmuss, D., Namerow, P., & Bauer, U., "Short-term Consequences of Parenting Versus Adoption Among Young Unmarried Women," *Journal of Marriage & the Family*, 54, no.1

(1992): 80-90; Weir, K., "Developmental, Familial, and Peer Deterrents to Adoption Placement," *Adoption Quarterly*, 5, no.1 (2001): 45-64; Weir, K., "Promoting Adoption as a Solution to Teen Pregnancy: A Study and Model," *Journal of Law & Family Studies*, 5, no. 2 (2003); Waite, L., & Gallagher, M., *The Case for Marriage: Why Married People are Happier, Healthier, and Better Off Financially* (New York: Doubleday, 2000).

2. National Committee for Adoption, *1989 Abortion Factbook* (Washington, DC: NCFA, 989).

3. Bachrach, C., Stolley, K., & London, K., "Relinquishment of Premarital Births: Evidence fro National Survey Data," *Family Planning Perspectives*, 24 (1992): 26; Sobol M., & Daly, K., "The Adoption Alternative for Pregnant Adolescents: Decision Making, Consequences, and Policy Initiatives," *Journal of Social Issues*, 48, no. 3 (1992): 143-61. See note 1, Weir, 2001; Weir, 2003.

4. Nichols, M. & Schwartz, R. *Family Therapy: Concepts & Methods*, 7th ed. (Boston, MA: Pearson, 2006).

5. Ibid.

6. Weir, K., *Coming Out of the Adoptive Closet* (Lanham, MD: University Press of America, 2003).

7. Benson, P., Sharma, A., & Roehlkepartain, E. *Growing Up Adopted* (Minneapolis: Search Institute, 2004).

8. Miller, R., "Do children make a marriage unhappy?" *Marriage and Families*, April 2001, 13-18.

9. Weir, K., "The Magnifying Effect: The Recursive Benefits of Marriage and Adoption Throughout the Adoptive Family Life-Cycle," *Journal of Law & Family Studies*, 6, no.1 (2004).

10. Weir, K., "Developmental Predictors of Seeking Family Therapy Among Adoptive Families: A Comparison of Individual and Family Developmental Needs," (under review).

11. Brodzinsky, D., Schechter, M., & Henig, R., *Being Adopted: The Lifelong Search for Self* (New York: Doubleday, 1992), 4.

12. Erikson, E., *Childhood and Society* (New York: W.W. Norton & Company, 1950).

13. Curtis, J., *Tell Me Again About the Night I Was Born* (New York: Harper Collins, 1996).

14. Campbell, S., *Behavior Problems in Preschool Children: Clinical and Developmental Issues* (New York: Guilford Press, 2002).

15. Tucker, A., Dinges D., & Van Dongen, H., "The Interindividual Differences in the Sleep Physiology of Young Healthy Adults," *Journal of Sleep Research*, 16 (2007): 170-80.

16. See note 11.

17. Ibid.

18. Ibid., 172.

19. Ternay, M., Wilborn B., & Day H., "Perceived Child-Parent Relationships and Child Adjustment in Families with Both Adopted and Natural Children," *Genetic Psychology*, 146, no.2 (1985): 261-72.

Chapter Ten: Post-Adoption Therapy Services

1. Strong, T., Sutherland, O., Couture, S., Godard, G, & Hope, T., "Karl Tomm's Collaborative Approaches to Counselling," *Canadian Journal of Counseling*, 42, no.3 (2008): 174-191.

2. Child Welfare Information Gateway, Adoption Assistance for Children Adopted From Foster Care (Washington, DC: U.S. Department of Health and Human Services, June 2004), http://www.childwelfare.gov/pubs/sp_subsid.cfm (accessed November 2, 2010).

3. Axline, V., *Dibs In Search of Self* (Boston: Houghton Mifflin, 1964).

4. Landreth, G., *Play Therapy: The Art of the Relationship* (New York: Taylor & Francis Books, 2002).

5. Carmichael, K., *Play Therapy: An Introduction* (Upper Saddle River, NJ: Pearson Education, 2006), 105.

6. Ibid.

7. Jernberg, A. & Booth, P., *Theraplay: Helping Parents and Children Build Better Relationships Through Attachment-Based Play*, 2nd ed., (San Francisco, Jossey-Bass, 1999).

8. Rubin, P. & Tregay, J., *Play with Them: Theraplay Groups in Classrooms* (Springfield, IL: Charles C. Thomas, 1989); Weir, K., "Using Integrative Play Therapy with Adoptive Families to Treat Reactive Attachment Disorder: A Case Example," *Journal of Family Psychotherapy*, 18, no. 4 (2007): 1-16.

9. Weir, K., "Repairing Adoptive and Foster Attachments," *Family Therapy Magazine*, 5, no. 5 (Sept.-Oct. 2006): 17-20.

10. Fivas-Depeursinge, E., "Documenting Time-Bound Circular View of Hierarchies: A Micro-Analysis of Parent-Infant Dyadic Interaction," *Family Process*, 30 (1991): 101-20.

11. Broderick, C., *Marriage and the Family*, 4th ed., (Englewood Cliffs, NJ: Prentice Hall, 1992).

12. Hughes, D., *Attachment-Focused Family Therapy* (New York: W.W. Norton & Company, 2007).

13. Ibid., 14.

14. Ibid., 62.

15. Goffmna, E., *The Presentation of Self in Everyday Life* (New York: Pantheon Books, 1959).

16. See note 11.

17. Rogers, C., *On Becoming A Person* (Boston: Houghton Mifflin, 1961).

18. See note 11, p. 68.

19. See note 11, p.82.

20. See note 11, p. 76.

21. See note 11, p. 87.

22. Nichols, M. & Schwartz R., *Family Therapy: Concepts & Models*, 7th ed. (Boston: Pearson, 2006). Here nonverbal attunement is akin to Minuchin's structural family therapy model.

23. See note 7, Weir, 2007.

24. Beck, A., Cognitive Therapy and the Emotional Disorders (New York, Penguin Books, 1979); Ellis, A., *Overcoming Destructive Beliefs, Feelings, and Behaviors: New Directions for Rational Emotive Behavior Therapy* (Amherst, NY: Prometheus Books, 2001); Ellis, A. & Harper, R., *A Guide to Rational Living.* (Hollywood: Wilshire Book Company, 1997); Ellis, A. & MacLaren, C., *Rational Emotive Behavior Therapy: A Therapist's Guide*, 2nd ed. (Atascadero, CA: Impact Publishers, 2005); Jacobson, N. & Gurman, eds., *Clinical Handbook of Couple Therapy* (New York: Guilford Press, 1995); Dattilio, F. & Epstein, N., "Introduction to the Special Section: The Role of Cognitive-Behavioral Interventions in Couple and Family Therapy," *Journal of Marital and Family Therapy*, 31, no. 1 (2005): 7-13; Reinecke, M., Dattilio, F., & Freeman, A., eds. *Cognitive Therapy with Children and Adolescents: A Casebook for Clinical Practice* (New York: Guilford Press, 2006).

25. See note 23, Ellis & MacLaren, 2005; Ellis, 2001.

26. Skinner, B., *The Behavior of Organisms: An Experimental Analysis* (Acton, MA: Copley Publishing Group, 1938); id., *Walden Two* (Indianapolis: Hackett Publishing Company, 1948); id., *Verbal Behavior* (Acton, MA: Copley Publishing Group, 1957); id., *Beyond Freedom and Dignity* (Indianapolis, IN: Hackett Publishing Company, 1971).

27. See note 21.

28. Barth, R., Crea, T., John, K., Thoburn, J., & Quinton, D., "Beyond Attachment Theory and Therapy: Towards Sensitive and Evidence-based Interventions with Foster and Adoptive Families in Distress," *Child and Family Social Work*, 10, (2005): 257-68.

29. Weir, K., "Repairing Adoptive and Foster Attachments," *Family Therapy Magazine*, 5, no. 5 (Sept./Oct., 2006): 17-20

30. White, M. & Epston, D., *Narrative Means to Therapeutic Ends* (New York: W.W. Norton & Co., 1990).

31. See note 21.

32. Weir, K., *Coming Out of the Adoptive Closet* (Lanham, MD: University Press of America, 2003).

33. Ibid.

34. Besa, D., "Evaluating Narrative Family Therapy Using Single-System Research Designs," *Research on Social Work Practice*, 4, no.3 (2004): 309-25. Etchison, M. & Kliest, D., "Review of Narrative Therapy: Research and Utility," *The Family Journal*, 8, no.1 (2000): 61-6. Larner, G., "Family Therapy and the Politics of Evidence," *Journal of Family Therapy*, 26 (2004): 17-39. Sprenkle, D., "Effectiveness Research in Marriage and Family Therapy," Alexandria, VA: American Association for Marriage and Family Therapy, 2002.

34. Child Welfare Information Gateway, "Post-adoption Services: A Factsheet for Families," (Washington, DC: U.S. Department of Health and Human Services, 2006), http://www.childwelfare.gov/pubs/f_postadoption.cfm (accessed Nov.2, 2010).

Chapter Eleven: Why We Need More Adoptions

1. U.S. Department of Health and Human Services, Administration for Children and Families, Children's Bureau, "AF-

CARS Report #17: Preliminary Estimates for FY 2009," http://www.acf.hhs.gov/programs/cb/stats_research/afcars/tar/report10.htm (accessed October 25, 2010).

2. Weir, K., *Coming Out of the Adoptive Closet* (Lanham, MD: University Press of America, 2003).

Glossary

Adjusted age. The developmental age of a prematurely born child based on his due date rather than the actual date of birth. It's sometimes called the corrected age or gestational age and helps professionals determine if developmental delays are related to lack of gestational growth or other factors affecting development.

Adoption plan. The individualized plan of the birth parents explaining what type of adoption experience they desire for the child. The plan outlines details such as whether they want an open or closed adoption, the family structure (e.g., two parents vs. single parent, martial status, sexual orientation), any religious preferences, and details about contact with the adoptive parents.

Adoption triad. The three primary sets of people affected by the adoption experience: the birth parents, the adoptive parents, and the adopted child.

Asynchronous development. Human development is comprised of several dimensions linked to but not entirely dependent on chronological age, such as physical development and cognition. Whenever one dimension or set of dimensions is significantly more advanced than others, developmental theorists apply this term. For example, gifted children may have higher than expected cognitive development for their age, but lower than average social or emotional development.

Closed adoption. An adoption in which contact and information exchange between the birth parents and adoptive parents is minimal or nonexistent.

Commoditization of adoptive children. A figurative economic device used to describe the market forces of supply and demand as applied to the availability of adoptable children. In an abstract sense, children become the "commodity," equipped with varying traits that help or hinder their chance of being adopted. Those traits include aspects such as age, health, race, history of abuse or neglect, and prenatal history. Younger, healthier children with clean histories and the same racial background as the seeking adoptive parents are preferred; however, they are less available than children of an older age, children with medical concerns, drug-exposure, or a history of abuse, and children of color sought by adoptive parents not of the same race. This makes children and their traits a "commodity" that affects the length of wait-time for an available child as well as the financial cost.

Concurrent planning. In U.S. child welfare systems, foster parents generally receive two parallel plans when a child is placed in their home. The preferred plan is for the child to be reunited with his birth family. The secondary plan is for the foster parents to adopt the child. Thus, at the same time foster parents work toward reunification with the birth parents, they make a contingency adoption plan should reunification with birth family fail to materialize. This can be a source of emotional strain on the couple playing these dual roles, but it typically allows for faster adoptions and more secure attachments. Reducing delays in permanency family placements, it places the interests of the child first. It is sometimes informally referred to as a "fast-track" adoption.

Cultural competency. A sufficient measure of training, experience, and regard for dissimilar cultures such that a professional can provide services in a culturally respectful and sensitive way. For adoptive parents considering adopting a child outside of their cultural background, this may also refer to childrearing that preserves the child's understanding of and connection to his original heritage.

Deinstitutionalization. The process of a large-standing formalized segment of society becoming more flexible, open, responsive, and diversified. Orphanages represent a historically institutionalized approach to adoption. Recent trends have showed signs of adoption practices turning toward a more diversified way of meeting the needs of children and families. As society deinstitutionalizes adoption, adoptive families have more freedom but also more uncertainty.

Family system. The people who make up a family, sometimes restricted to those who share a household or are related by blood, marriage, or adoption. More inclusive definitions suggest that self-determination (i.e., whomever the family says is the family is the family) and mutual recognition are sufficient for membership.

Family systems theory. A model for understanding family behavior that emphasizes boundaries, reciprocal interaction, and the recognition that "the whole is greater than the sum of its parts." According to family systems theory, individuals do not live in isolation and, accordingly, our thoughts, feelings, and actions are shaped through recursive human interaction.

This therapeutic framework may be beneficial for adoptive families due to the expanded networks (e.g., birth family systems, adoptive family systems, school systems, foster care systems, court systems) they tend to occupy.

Formal adoption (or formal kinship adoption). A legally authorized adoption entered into by the extended family or kinship system.

Home study. Part of the adoption process requires a thorough review of prospective adoptive families, family members residing in the home, and domestic conditions in order to determine if the family is suitable for adoption. This may take from a few weeks to as long as six months. Generally,the following are required:

- A written report detailing the family's background, history, financial status, and house plan
- Letters of reference from associates
- Screening interviews conducted by a social worker of the couple and any other people, including children, living in the home
- Adoption coursework and training
- A criminal background check of any adults residing in the home
- Home inspection to ensure compliance with the licensing state's foster care laws and regulations

Informal adoption. A form of kinship adoption that may or may not be legally recognized such as grandparents adopting their grandchild through the child welfare system. These tend to occur more frequently among families of color.

Intensive Treatment Foster Care (ITFC). A program offering increased professional and foster parent attention for foster children with serious emotional and behavioral problems. Children are referred through child welfare agencies and subcontracting agencies known as Foster Family Agencies. The child is typically placed in a home where they are the only child. Due to the expense of increased services, ITFC limits the number of children who can be designated for services. It is often used as a last resort before placement into a group home, or as a transition out of a residential placement and back into foster care.

Leap-frogging. When infertile couples feel as though they are lagging behind their social counterparts who are having children but catch up once they adopt, this is called leap-frogging. It describes the raid transition adoptive couples experience from a family life-cycle perspective.

Life chances. The German sociologist Max Weber used this term to describe the probability that a person will have the opportunity to improve the conditions of her life. In an adoption context, we can use Weber's life chances not only to describe the odds that a child will be adopted, but also how adoption will influence the quality of the child's life given her history, background, and physiological traits.

Magnifying effect. An amplification of the satisfaction or strain felt in adoptive family relationships when the family transitions through life-cycle stages. Couples who have problems before they marry will have even larger problems after they marry; couples with steady, loving marriages before they adopt will find the transition into parenthood enhances the strength of their marriage.

Method of adoption. The means through which the couple adopts a child. The following are examples:

- **Designated:** When the birth parents and prospective adoptive parents decide to make an adoption plan together, this is called designated adoption. Often it happens via social contacts or through the Internet. Depending on the reliability of the source, it may or may not carry elevated risk for fraud or the dissolution of the adoption.

- **Independent:** Adopting through a professional such as a doctor or lawyer, many of whom specialize in facilitating adoption. Often independent adoption providers are hired to finalize the legal procedures required for designated adoptions or kinship adoptions.

- **International:** Adopting a child from outside of the Unites States. This is usually done through an agency specializing in a particular country or region.

- **Kinship:** Any adoption by a relative in the family or extended family is considered a kinship adoption. It may occur legally or without formal licensure. Increasing numbers of grandparents and step-parents are adopting children.

- **Private Agency:** Adopting through an agency that facilitates adoptions and is not affiliated with government. These often are non-profit organizations and religiously affiliated agencies.

- **Public Agency:** Adopting through the child welfare system—a government-run program offering foster care services to children who have been abused, neglected, or otherwise do not have a suitable home or family. Many of these children are older, have special needs, or are children of color.

Narrative family therapy. A model of therapy that presumes the client's life is like a story with multiple meanings. If we change how the client "reads" their life story and events within that life story, we can change how he thinks, feels, and acts. One of several effective models in treatment of adopted children and their families, it presumes that words and perceptions are powerful instruments of change. As a language-oriented therapy, it applies the following specialized definitions:

- **Deconstructing destructive cultural assumptions:** One of the main causes for problems, according to narrative family therapists, is that people accept certain societal or cultural assumptions without questioning them. Narrative family therapists seek to "deconstruct" such myths, so the client may transcend cultural expectations and do what is right for himself and his family.
- **Externalizing the problem:** A tendency for families to engage in infighting and lay blame on each other when interpersonal problems occur. When working with families, narrative family therapists attempt to separate the person from the problem. The goal is to reduce shame by redirecting the family's energies toward finding solutions rather than defending themselves against attacks.
- **Problem-saturated stories:** Sometimes people focus obsessively on their problems and let these dominate their life's story. Narrative family therapists seek to reframe problem-saturated stories, suggesting alternative interpretations that are more positive.
- **Reauthoring the whole story:** The creation of a different interpretation of the client's life's story, in order to increase his agency in enacting change. The therapist tries to reinforce the story with key insights that support the client's new way of thinking.
- **Relative influence questions:** When a therapist tries to ascertain the client's perception of her ability to change her own life, this is called a relative influence question. A classic relative influence question is "Who's in charge here—the person or the problem?"
- **Restory:** Helping clients to create a different interpretation of their life's story. A narrative family therapist might help an adopted child who believes her birth mother didn't want her by presenting the family history in an optimistic light: the birth mother, in spite of the difficulties in her own life, loved the child enough to find her a good home.
- **Unique outcomes:** Looking for exceptions to a problem, the therapist might ask, "Has there been a time when this problem didn't occur? What's different about those times?" By focusing on times when the problem wasn't as persistent or troubling, the therapist and

client may discover strengths that can be expanded upon to alleviate personal hang-ups.

Open adoption. Adoption that allows for contact and information exchange between the birth parents and adoptive parents. On the adoption continuum there are varying degrees of openness, from exchanging pictures and making occasional house visits to forging a close-knit, ongoing relationship.

PACE: playfulness, acceptance, curiosity, and empathy (or PLACE—adding love). Daniel Hughes, a clinical psychologist, developed a treatment model called Dyadic Developmental Psychotherapy (DDP) that is highly effective in treating adopted and foster children. In the DDP model, Hughes recommends that therapists working with children use the four caregiving postures established in PACE. He later added "love" as fifth treatment dimension.

Permanency planning. Under the Adoption and Safe Families Act of 1997, states and child welfare systems are given incentives for ensuring that each foster child has a plan for a permanent home. Generally, those plans include reunification with birth family, legal guardianship, or adoption.

Primary infertility. When a couple has not been able to conceive a child or carry to a child to full term through biological means, it is called primary infertility.

Rapid transition to parenthood. Whenever a couple enters into parenthood, they experience significant life-cycle transitions. Typically a couple has about nine months to plan and prepare for a new baby. With adoption, couples may have far less time to prepare for a new child. Sometimes couples find therapy helpful, especially if they are feeling guilt because they "ought to" be excited about adopting but instead are experiencing fear and unexpected strain on their relationships.

Reactive attachment disorder (RAD). The clinical diagnosis therapists frequently apply to children who are experiencing difficulty forming secure attachments with caregivers. It occurs more frequently in adoptive and foster families than in other types of families due to the children's separation histories. Criteria include onset of symptoms before age five, chronic socialization problems, and abusive or neglectful care, and results in behavior problems.

Secondary infertility. When a couple has been able to have biological children in the past but cannot conceive a child or carry a child to full-term, this is known as secondary infertility.

Systems theory. Marriage and family therapists (MFTs) often take what is called a systems theory perspective in understanding how families operate. Instead of looking to assign individual blame or pathology, they try to see where relationships are not functioning well and repair areas of conflict. MFTs locate the child's development in the context of the family, focusing on how children balance a need for autonomy with a desire for family cohesion. From a theoretical perspective, the theory presupposes that systems strive for equilibrium (homeostasis); that in systems the whole is greater than the sum of its parts (non-summativity); that systems maintain boundaries; and that systems change over time.

Theraplay. A specific type of play therapy developed by the clinical psychologist Ann Jernberg that focuses on enhancing parent/child attachment along four dimensions:
- **Challenge:** As parents and children face and overcome chal-

lenges by working together they grow closer. Helping a child stretch themselves by facing and successfully overcoming challenges helps them to develop, progress, and feel good about themselves.

• **Engagement:** Attunement to a child in an upbeat, positive, and playful way. Often involving good eye contact, it helps the child feel he is being paid attention to and is important to the parent.

• **Nurture:** Tenderness communicated to a child by a parent through appropriate physical touch and affection. Nurturing implies attending to a child's pain, whether physical or emotional. Feeding games often are used in therapy as a way of aiding the parent in taking care of the children and facilitating appropriate touch.

• **Structure:** Appropriate limit-setting that provides the child with a sense of security. When the parent takes charge, it communicates to the child that the parent loves him enough to help and protect him.

Wallowing. Therapists must "wallow," meaning they must empathize with the pain and difficulties in their clients' lives, in order to provide insight and support. That is part of why therapists are vulnerable to burnout if they do not practice good self-care. Equally important is a therapist's ability to help clients make measurable changes in their lives. Producing a lot of insight and gaining a better understanding of the meaning of client's problems without promoting actual, concrete behavioral change does not help a client and may exacerbate his frustrations. Therapists can facilitate change in a variety of ways such as teaching clients strategies for de-escalating confrontation and improving relationships with other family members. Therapists who can both wallow with and facilitate change in their clients are superior to mediocre therapists who can do only one or the other.

Index